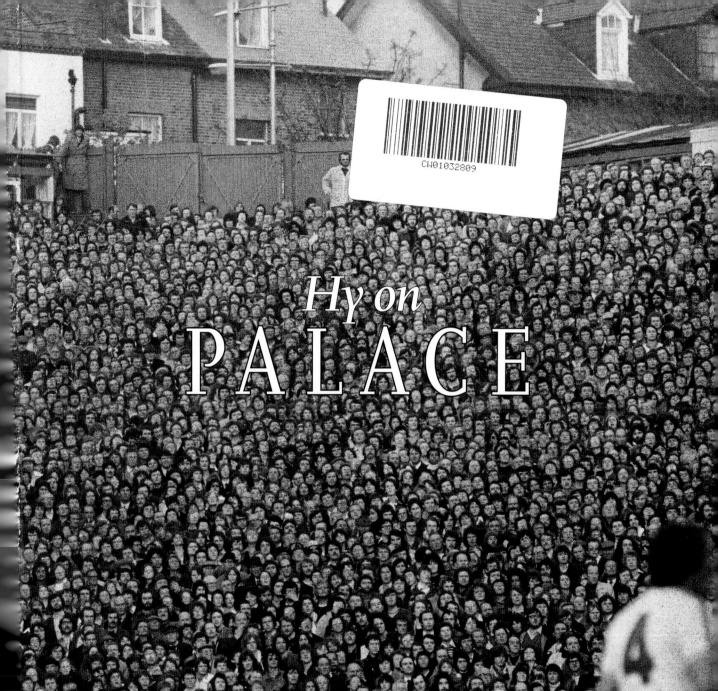

*Hy on*
# PALACE

# *Hy on* PALACE

 Crystal Palace fans Centenary Publishing

Text and Design ©2005 CPfCP and Photographs ©2005 Hy Money

First published in 2005 by
Crystal Palace fans' Centenary Publishing
P.O. Box 2005, London SE25 5EN
cpfcp2005@hotmail.com

Crystal
Palace
fans'
Centenary
Publishing

ISBN 0 85667 617 9 (softcover)
ISBN 0 85667 618 7 (hardcover)

All photography, unless otherwise noted, by Hy Money

Project Management and Captions: Don Madgwick

Edited and Designed by Norman Turpin

Many thanks to all those, including David Payne, who gave invaluable assistance with player identification.

"Glad All Over" Music and Words by Dave Clark and Mike Smith.
© Copyright 1963 Ivy Music Limited, 8/9 Frith Street, London W1D 3JB.
Reproduced by permission.  All rights reserved.
*Wishing you all every success* - Dave Clark

All photographs printed by Banstead Studio, Surrey

Reproduction, Printing and Binding by Craft Print, Singapore

### See Hy's website:
## www.hymoney.co.uk

You can find further background information, as well as Hy's anecdotes to these photographs at the Crystal Palace fans' Centenary Project web site at:

www.eagles100.org

Why not get involved and add your stories to the memory bank of recollections we're building to celebrate our Club's Centenary Year.

Don Rogers 1973. Photo by Tony Maberly of Radio Mayday

CONTENTS

Don Rogers 2005. Photo by Neil Witherow of Palace Echo

Bert and the steaming soup.

Church Parade at Lovedale school. Hy is the girl second from the right.
*(Photo courtesy of Ralph Leese)*

I FIRST CAUGHT SIGHT of him perched at the top of the stairs, eating soup from a china bowl; a cuddly sort of man with greying hair and a persona that seemed friendly and approachable. "So, you're Hy Money, the one who's been ringing all week asking if you can take photographs from the pitch." the man said, between slurps.

"That's me," I admitted, although I had no idea to whom I was speaking. "As no one returned my calls, I thought I'd come to ask personally. The Receptionist told me to go up to the Manager's Office so I'm on my way. "

I wanted to say "Excuse me please, let me pass." but he sat there, filling the space like he owned it.

"Why do you want to?" he asked, looking up at me quizzically. "Are you a Press photographer?"

"Er ... not exactly, but I so badly want to take photographs. It's hard to explain."

"Well" said the man, now straightening himself up, lumbering towards a room with MANAGER written on the door, "with a name like Hy Money and a cheek like yours ...". He called for someone whom I later learned to be the Club Secretary, and said "For heaven's sake, give this woman a Pass and get rid of her." "Yes, Mr. Head" came the terse reply as he left, eyebrows raised, to return moments later, handing me a small brown envelope bearing my name, and the rest ... can be found within the pages of this book.

### From Mamma to Mammarazzi

Right from the very beginning I was told (and hence believed it to be true) that photography was mans' work. So it was down to my husband as owner of a camera to photograph our first-born child Lisa so that I could introduce her (in pictures at least) to family and friends who still lived in

India. Weeks turned to months and still no snaps, and what with the start of the cricket season when you wouldn't see his heels for dust, it was time for drastic action. In desperation, I dug out the Box Brownie camera my mother had given me when I left India's shores, and decided it was time to experiment.

The man from the chemist where I had gone to buy a film explained the procedure for loading it into the camera. Poised for action, I surprised myself by noticing the smallest detail that might have distracted the eye away from my subject. It was not enough to just capture Lisa's likeness. Instead, I wafted into another world where what mattered was that the image also caught the essence of my child, and, to that end, my patience knew no bounds. All too soon, the 12-exposure film came to an end and I suffered the endless wait of 10 days for the film to be processed. Nothing could equal the magic of opening the package to see for the first time if what you saw in your mind's eye matched the photograph. There she was, so pretty and cute, and a great sense of artistic achievement washed over me.

Dividing the photos, I air-mailed some to India then boldly took a pair of scissors to the remaining few to snip and paste them on to the first page of a photo album and – Hey Presto! A photographer was born. It would take weeks before I could skim off a few pence from housekeeping money to save for my next roll of film.

The open sided 'Toy Train' in the Nilgiris Hills of south-west India. *(Photo courtesy of Ralph Leese)*

*India Days*

Sending me by ocean liner to a foreign land was not the first time I had embarked on an epic journey into the unknown. Years earlier, aged eight, and this time accompanied by my mother, we set off for my first day at boarding school (later joined by my two younger sisters). We had to use a network of trains, including the Overnight Express from Bangalore and the open sided 'Toy Train' that chugged and meandered its stately way up

BELOW LEFT: Lisa as a baby: "My first attempt at photography."

BELOW: Palace team collage 1972-73. "My first year as Palace photographer and the players get the same snip-and-paste treatment."

Christmas Day, Bombay: "My mother (top right in this photo), my two sisters and I (bottom right, clutching my Box Brownie) pose for a photo before heading off to the harbour. There I boarded a steamer on a one-way ticket to Blighty, my only possessions being a tin trunk containing warm clothes, the address of a Croydon boarding-house, fifteen pounds cash and, of course, the camera my mother had given me as a Christmas present. Ahead of me was the daunting prospect of starting a new life amongst total strangers and adapting to drastic changes in climate, culture and currency."

the mountainside at a walking pace, via 16 tunnels, to our final destination, Lovedale, in the Nilgiris Hills of south-western India. Being left there alone, at the end of the 14-hour journey, was a traumatic experience that only lessened as the years rolled by.

The Lawrence Memorial Royal Military School in Lovedale was situated 7,500 feet above sea level within its own grounds of 800 acres, amidst eucalyptus-clad hillsides. Created in 1858 by Major General Sir Henry Lawrence for children of British Military personnel serving in India in those early days of the British Raj, the re-creation of the British Public School system transported itself admirably to the temperate climate of India's Hill Station, away from the scorching heat of the cities, sufficiently satisfying the needs of parents who, having the best of both worlds, no longer needed to send their offspring thousands of miles back home to be similarly schooled.

Unfortunately, Sir Henry did not see the completion of this, the last of his four schools in the Hill Stations across India, having been at the receiving end of a loose cannon defending the city of Lucknow during the Indian Mutiny. He took two days to slowly bleed to death and his dying words "I tried to do my duty" were recorded for posterity in the history books about the British Empire, but more importantly they became embedded in the school folklore as an inspiration for all of us who revered him as our Founder.

Wearing khaki uniforms (navy on Sundays) we marched in columns of three to the beat of the school military band and saluted the King's colours. We learned rifle shooting and the school once held the record for the highest score in the British Empire! Latin, French, Shakespeare, and the works of the world's greatest artists and composers were all part of our classical education along with an emphasis on sport. Academically the ultimate aim was to achieve flying colours in the Senior Cambridge School Certificate Examinations.

For some of us the distance home was too great to travel, except for Christmas and the summer holidays, so Lovedale became home as well as school. I had to acclimatise myself to institutional life. We slept 30 to each dormitory, co-existing as harmoniously as possible. Above all we learnt at a very early age to abide steadfastly by the rules so as to lead a punishment-free life. Any sign of individuality that might raise its head above the parapet was only to be attempted by the brave hearted, which did not include me.

Cameras: "For those interested in the cameras I used, the first was the Box Brownie (this page, top left) then the Rolleiflex (above), which was very ill-suited to football photography (as I had to change film every 12 exposures!), before I eventually turned to 35mm Nikon equipment, which I have now used for more than 30 years (left).

There I remained until, aged seventeen-and-a-half, it was off with the uniforms and out with the pigtails. Ringing in our ears as we left was the hymn at final assembly "Lord dismiss us with Thy Blessing" and a reminder from the Head Master that we should be privileged to call ourselves "Lawrencians" and should go out into the world with high standards of conduct and accept responsibility for our actions. Our motto "NEVER GIVE IN" would always be there as a reminder that nothing is impossible if you try hard enough. Soon it was time to board the 'Toy Train' for the start of the final journey home. Still basking in the afterglow of the British Raj, giddy days were ahead. For me it was now time to be a girl in a pretty dress and open-toed, high-heeled shoes, taking a rickshaw ride down Bangalore's Mahatma Ghandi Road, to see and be seen. Time to take 4 o'clock High Tea at the Club, swim in the river, play croquet on the lawn and later, picnic by moonlight. Time to fox trot at the Tea Dance or sample the magic of the movies. The film only changed once every two months but brought Hollywood into our lives so that we could experiment with Rita Hayworth lips and Ava Gardner hairstyles and fall madly in love with James Dean. Unburdened by rules and freed from a life cocooned in a bubble of seclusion, the future beckoned with seductive arms.

Then came the bombshell!

The first clue to impending disaster came by post with the arrival of a pillow-case stuffed full of wool, accompanied by a set of knitting needles. The hard facts were spelt out in a letter from my mother who had remarried and moved thousands of miles away to Cawnpore, somewhere in the vastness that is India. Her new husband, a Textile Chemist from Accrington, Lancashire, had spent all his working life in India's cotton mills. He had kindly provided the funds to drip-feed our exodus to England in search of a better life, away from the turbulence of post-independent India. I had six weeks notice to knit warm clothes for the Christmas Day departure and arrival in mid-winter England. My mother promised that when her husband was due for retirement (within three years), we would all be re-united. Ever obedient, I knew the matter would not be open to discussion and with each row of two plain/two purl, I accepted my fate in silent resignation.

### Life in England

Bereft of family and the familiarity of people I had grown up with, and still feeling a stranger in a foreign land, a proposal of marriage seemed the answer to a maiden's prayer. We'd met on my birthday when the girls at work took me to a dance at the Orchid Ballroom in Purley. We were married 7 months later, creating a family of four children within six-and-a-half years. Now, with my own little dynasty not only in the same country but also under the same roof, I felt it was time to put down roots with

ABOVE: "Me with Lisa, Anthony, Martin and Stuart on Brighton Pier, photographed by the 'Monkey Man'.

BELOW: Lisa on the beach: "With my Rolleiflex, I was able to take better photographs and couldn't resist capturing Lisa dancing on the beach."

RIGHT: "Instead of saying 'smile please' I say 'jump please' as I snap Lisa leaping off the garden wall. My desire for action photography had already taken root."

ABOVE AND BELOW: "A typical sight after a game of football in the back garden as Martin and Stuart come in at close of play, caked in mud. Little did I realise then that one day I would photograph a similarly mud-splattered professional footballer (John Burridge)."

dreams of India dissolved so far into the distance as to have no more relevance in my life.

Like most families of my generation, our children did not attend playgroups or nursery school but spent every day and all day together, until each in turn reached school age. Added to this, my husband, whom I had known to be a sports fanatic during our courting days, continued his passion to play football, cricket and snooker. So with neither his company nor his help, and no extended family for support, life for me was edge-to-edge busy.

### The Birthday Treat

At the time of 'the' Birthday treat, Stuart had started school. The last little sparrow had finally flown the nest and it was time to take on a part-time job, if only to counter the loneliness of an empty house. Lacking in self-confidence after almost 13 years mired in domesticity, I dipped my toes into the workplace by volunteering my services at the local Oxfam, whilst my second job involved taking a couple of local ladies back-and-forth from their homes to the 'Over-60s Club', also on the High Street, doing bits of shopping for them, making use of the fact that I had passed my driving test.

Photography was still my passion and provided a creative release from day-to-day life and a joyful means of chronicling my childrens' progress over the years. My husband, aware of the limitations of the Box Brownie, bought me a second hand Rolleiflex camera, giving me greater scope for taking better pictures.

Around this time, Martin announced that he wished to go to the Palace as his 7th birthday treat. I tried to dissuade him saying we couldn't guarantee that the Queen would be there. "Not THAT Palace, silly," he said, exasperated. "I mean CRYSTAL Palace. It's a football club."

My chin hit the curb at the mention of the 'F' word. Due to my husband's obsession with sport, football (or any sport) was not my favourite topic of conversation. The thought of venturing out into the unknown world of football terrified me. It was so far removed from the comfort zone of my environment that no amount of Motherly Love could fortify me to take on the task. Biding my time, I tactfully mentioned that it

should be the privilege of a father to take his children to their first professional game, especially as it was as a birthday treat and yes, it would mean sacrificing cricket for just one day, but with several weeks notice to make the arrangements, he finally agreed to fill the role.

*The Match*

Come the day of the match, the excitement was tangible. Dressed in their replica soccer shirts and with Martin's best friend Tony in tow, the boys spent the morning clock-watching, anxiously waiting for the big adventure to begin. Crystal Palace were playing at home to Liverpool. Apparently, this was a 'big fixture' and couldn't have been a more spectacular event for a first outing into the world of professional football.

Then came a phone call which my husband dealt with, returning to ask me "are my whites ready?"

I thought I had misheard but he asked again. By the time the implication of the question had sunk in, he was upstairs packing his cricket bag. He mumbled something like "They're one man short. What's the big deal, you'll just have to take them."

Accompanied by Martin's moan "I don't want to go with Mum, she hates football," he handed me the tickets, the A-to-Z and the address of the Crystal Palace Football Club, before walking out into the sunshine for his game of cricket.

I felt sick with the responsibility suddenly thrust upon me. Where is this place called Selhurst Park? How do I get there? What about the crowds? What if I get lost? What if I have a crash 'cos I'm dithering about trying to find where I'm going? Where do I park? What if I lose one of the boys in the throng and what is to become of Lisa, as there was no ticket for her? All sorts of questions raged through my mind. The thought of

ABOVE: "Anthony making a flying save in goal during his school football match. 'Jacko' in flight during training at Selhurst Park."

"Martin, Anthony, Tony and Stuart all togged out in their Palace shirts ready for their trip to Selhurst Park."

ABOVE RIGHT: "My useless attempt to capture the action on the pitch from my seat in the stands. This made me determined that the next time, I would be sitting on the touchline."

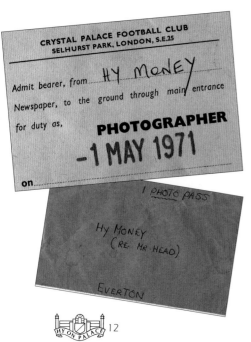

CRYSTAL PALACE FOOTBALL CLUB
SELHURST PARK, LONDON, S.E.25

Admit bearer, from .... HY MONEY

Newspaper, to the ground through main entrance

for duty as, **PHOTOGRAPHER**

**-1 MAY 1971**

on ....

1 PHOTO PASS

HY MONEY
(RE. MR HEAD)

EVERTON

venturing beyond the normal parameters of my driving world into unknown territory had me ventilating on the verge of a panic attack.

Flapping about helplessly, I phoned Tony's dad, "Please can you help?", but he owned a shop and couldn't leave at such short notice. Who else did I know? Who else could help? The answer? No one. So it was time to think about Sir Henry and "NEVER GIVE IN". With Lisa farmed out at her friend's house, and the A-to-Z opened at the appropriate page, thus began the 3rd most epic journey of my life. Once again it was not of my choosing and it was just as nerve-wracking as the previous two. This time it was neither an ocean liner nor the Overnight Express train. It was a little green Hillman Imp, loaded with four children and a Rolleiflex. With me at the helm, we ventured into the unknown, to a place called Selhurst Park, and no one was happy.

It was a few miles into our journey that I became aware of the steady stream of traffic all heading in one direction and at a snail's pace. It sometimes didn't move at all for long periods, allowing me to abandon the A-to-Z and just follow the car in front of me at a leisurely pace as it became obvious that all the traffic was Palace-bound, and soon the floodlight towers at the stadium acted as welcoming landmarks in the far distance.

The nearer we got to the ground, the more my spirits soared and by the time I arrived and miraculously found a place to park (thank you, God!) I felt a sudden flush of amazement that I had stretched myself beyond the barriers of my perceived limitations and survived.

Huddling together, our little group became part of the river of humanity floating as if on a conveyor belt, both sides of the pavement leading to the ground crammed to capacity, a flowing river like pilgrims to Mecca. Young and old, kids on their dad's shoulders, young couples holding hands, groups of noisy lads chanting in gravelly voices, elderly ladies wearing bobble caps festooned with rosettes and matching scarves, trying to keep up with the desperate pace of the flow, the streets awash in a ribbon of claret and blue. Fried onions from the hot dog stands tantalised the appetite, souvenir stall holders yelled their wares and uniformed police and club officials, attempting to marshall people, good-naturedly flexed their muscles. Not since I left the hubble and bubble of Bangalore had I seen so much commotion. It was as if I had stepped back in time to a long since forgotten life and I filled my lungs with the atmosphere.

Inside the stadium, the pleasure heightened at the sight of the large swathe of green grass encircled by a wall of terracing and seating where the Liverpool fans waved their bright red scarves besides the claret and blue of the Palace supporters. Like Dorothy in the Wizard of Oz, my world had exploded from black and white into glorious technicolour.

Accompanied by a gladiatorial roar from the crowds in anticipation of the countdown to the match, out stepped the Palace Dollies to form a guard of honour, the loudspeakers belting out the tune "Glad all Over", accompanied by huge banks of voices joining in, and those near the advertising boards banged them in rhythm with the music.

Another even louder, tribal roar heralded a long line of players emerging from the darkness of the tunnel, their scrunching studs echoing on the concrete floor. The steady stream of both team's players burst into the sunshine. Some went to the left, some to the right and the men in black went straight on. The stage was set for a duel and I was in thrall of what lay ahead.

The whistle blew and battle commenced. With my camera at the ready, and from the lofty perch of our seats, I just had to take photographs of the action on the pitch but the rows of peoples' heads kept getting in the way and images of the players appeared miniscule in my viewfinder. The frustra-

BELOW: "I would often take my Box Brownie to school sports day or, as in this photograph, to my boys' football games at their Primary school, taking photos from the touchline. Thanks to Bert Head, but now with a Rolleiflex camera, I was able to take this picture from the touchline at Selhurst Park with 'Jacko' in mid-air."

ABOVE RIGHT: "My idea of a family group photo – my four children and their cousins running towards me in my back garden, with three year old Stuart making a valiant effort to keep up. Years later, I was at Selhurst Park to capture the the fleet-footed Palace lads at a training session."

Hy in the Green Room at the Richard and Judy show .

tion was strangling me. I wanted to leap over the crowds and be right there beside the goal as the 'keeper sprang waist high above the heads of those around him to pluck the ball from mid air. Click. There he was flying parallel to the ground as he made a spectacular save, but from my seat in the stands, all I could do was grind my teeth and sigh with envy at those people who were sitting so close to the pitch as to smell the sweat. Here were grown-ups doing exactly what my children had done as I had photographed them playing and now, the beauty and strength of the action, click, frozen in time, graceful like ballet dancers, shirts billowing, hair flying as a head whacks the ball. Click. Sweat captured in globules. I wanted, I needed to capture it all on film but the distance made it impossible.

It mattered not who lost or won. All I knew was that I just had to get back there again to be within spitting distance of the action. Nothing less would do. I had never wanted anything more and although I had no idea where this driving force came from, I knew that I would be on a mission to make it happen. I also knew for sure that this day, this experience, would change my life forever.

So, swiftly came the end to what had turned out to be a thrilling day and it was time to take the tired children home, but I knew I'd return. After some initial persistence, I have Bert Head to thank for authorising my first Press Pass, which allowed me my first footprints down my own "Yellow Brick Road". It would be paved with many adventures and interesting characters along the way and liberate me to finally make my own choices in life.

HY MONEY, *October 2005*

BYE BYE BLACKBURN 89

June 3rd, 1989. Ian Wright and Mark Bright in jubilant spirits, matching the mood of the crowd as Palace win the Play-Off Final against Blackburn Rovers. The deadly duo finished the season with a combined 48 League and Play-Off goals.

 16

BYE BYE BLACKBURN 89

LEFT: Ron Noades gives his promotion speech in the dressing room after getting a right royal soaking, as Alex Dyer looks on.

RIGHT: More cork-poppin' as Novello Noades steals a kiss from Ian Wright. Glenn Pennyfather and Dave Madden can be seen to the right.

BELOW: The great 'Satchmo' Wright, on top o' the world.

Palace were at last Back In The Big Time thanks to Steve Coppell's masterfully constructed team.

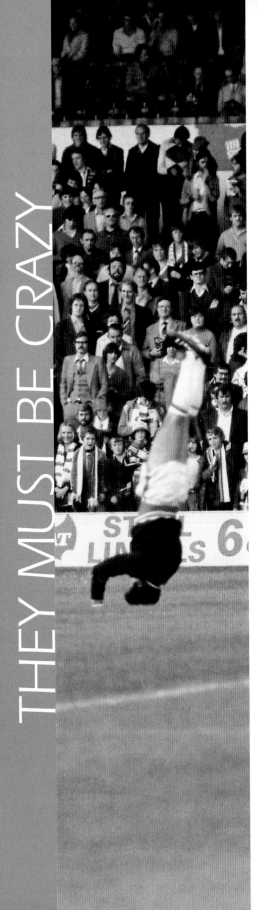

THEY MUST BE CRAZY

OPPOSITE, FAR LEFT: John Burridge praying to his own god.

All the other photos in this spread are devoted to arguably the finest Palace 'keeper of all time, John 'Jacko' Jackson. 'Jacko' was more responsible than any other individual player for sustaining Palace's four-year introductory spell in the old First Division. He was hugely popular with all Palace fans of the day and had he not been demoted by Malcolm Allison, Palace would most likely have retained their Second Division place instead of plunging directly into the dreaded old Third Division. Here, Hy not only captures his agility and bravery but also his intense disappointment at a rare moment of failure.

ABOVE, LEFT AND BELOW: Paul Hammond in full flight, grounded, and directing his defence.

RIGHT: Stretching as a shot clears the bar, David Fry was more limited in opportunities with the first team. He had been part of the Youth Cup winning side.

OPPOSITE PAGE: John 'Budgie' Burridge, whose 'daft as a brush' image belied the terrific professionalism he brought to the club. Hy captures him getting ready for his next mud bath, leaving the field with ex-Villa team mate Andy Gray and punching away against Wolves.

THEY MUST BE CRAZY

Paul Barron with Terry Gennoe, who played a few loan games for Palace in 1981. On the right Paul gets the best view in the house as one of the 83 goals shipped by the Palace defence that season flies into the net. Below he punches clear from Villa's Peter Withe.

ABOVE: The popular Perry Suckling (who later became goalkeeping coach at Spurs) salutes the fans.

TOP RIGHT: Andy Woodman is still a Palace fan. After leaving Palace he went on to save a penalty in a Play-Off Final at Wembley and co-author a book with Gareth Southgate.

BELOW AND RIGHT: Hy shoots Nigel Martyn enjoying two of the peak moments of his illustrious Palace career, at Wembley in 1990 and after promotion back to the top-flight as Champions in 1994.

THEY MUST BE CRAZY

YOU SAY THAT YOU YOU LOVE ME 70-71

LEFT: Mel Blyth, head and shoulders above the opposition.

ABOVE: An early photograph Hy took from pitch level. John McCormick joins Mel Blyth as they attack a corner kick against Everton. Steve Kember looks on and Alan Birchenall lurks behind Labone and Royle.

RIGHT: A great profile shot of Bobby Tambling as he runs to take another Palace corner, this time at the Whitehorse end.

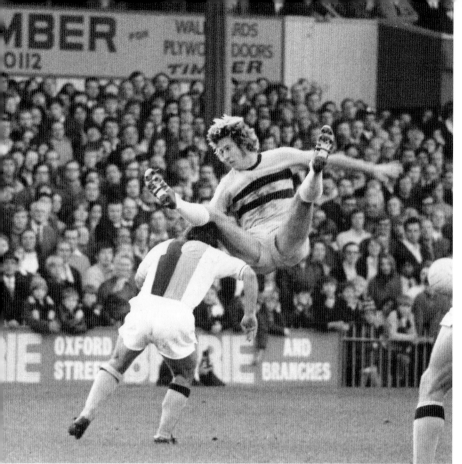

LEFT: "On me 'ead son". West Ham's Tommy Taylor is about to come down to earth over Bobby Kellard's back.

ABOVE AND BELOW LEFT: Kellard's industry was a major factor in the club's eventual survival.

ABOVE RIGHT: Bobby Tambling, Palace's top scorer in season 71-72, fires in a shot.

BELOW: Due to injury, John 'Yogi' Hughes made few appearances for Palace yet is well remembered. Here he teases a Leicester defender.

BELOW RIGHT: John McCormick at full stretch with George Best. Tony Taylor looks on.

ABOVE: It's Kung Fu fighting with Willie Wallace, who came to Palace having been a member of the Celtic team who were the first British winners of the European Cup in 1967.

LEFT AND RIGHT CENTRE: As one long-serving Glaswegian's important defensive role at Palace was coming to an end (John McCormick, left), so another one was about to begin. Jim Cannon, who is seen here in an early training shot, was to make a record 657 appearances for the club in 18 fantastic years of service.

FAR RIGHT: John Jackson drills the beanpole Ross Jenkins in a spot of old-fashioned man-to-man marking.

Very much an old fashioned, suited Manager, Bert Head's training sessions always aimed to build stamina. Among those huffing and puffing here are Peter Wall, David Payne, Bobby Kellard, John McCormick, Mel Blyth, Bobby

Goldthorpe, Ross Jenkins, Willie Wallace, Gerry Queen, Tony Taylor, John Jackson, John Craven and Alan Pinkney. Stepping up in the gym are Ross Jenkins, Willie Wallace and David Payne.

SWEAT AND TEARS

ABOVE: In this great sequence of Hy's fly-on-the-wall training photos, Malcolm Allison gets a quiet point across with Don Rogers, gives a specific group instruction, observes his prodigy Terry Venables picking up the coaching reins, then shares a lighter moment with Terry Long, himself a Palace legend. Long and Cannon represent 33 years of unbroken service with the club! Terry, despite still being registered as a player, never made his 1st Division debut but represented Palace in every other Division.

LEFT: Mal with Jim Cannon, Iain Phillip, Derek Possee and David Payne.

RIGHT MIDDLE: Mel Blyth and Roy Barry warm down on the terraces of the sunny Whitehorse Lane end.

BOTTOM RIGHT: At the Crystal Palace National Sports Centre Terry Venables pre-dates a John Harbin training routine.

SWEAT AND TEARS

ABOVE: Again at the CPNSC, Steve Perrin, Jim Cannon (JC) and Nicky Chatterton recover. TOP RIGHT: On the track, Ian 'Taff' Evans comes up on the outside of 'Jimbo' Cannon. BELOW: Coach Ernie Walley addresses Ian Evans, George Graham, Rachid 'Spider' Harkouk and Barry Silkman. RIGHT: George Graham and Phil Holder on the track, timed by Terry (far right).

LEFT: The marquee on the pitch is nothing new. Various key people in Palace's social scene over the years getting their glad (all over) rags on.
ABOVE AND BELOW: At another Palace function Chairman Ray Bloye, Manager Bert Head and Coach Terry Long join players including

SHAKEN – NOT STIRRED

Charlie Cooke, Bobby Tambling, Derek Possee, Don Rogers and Tony Taylor, all accompanied by their better halves.
RIGHT: Charlie Cooke starts spreading the news with the house band.
BOTTOM RIGHT: Bert, his wife and their daughter Sue.

SHAKEN — NOT STIRRED

LEFT: Hy visits the studio to capture the recording of 'Claret and Blue'. Among others at the microphone are Brian Simpson, Mickey Pratt, John Craven, Tony Taylor, Alan Pinkney and Jacko Jackson.

BELOW: Celebrating promotion at Cervantes in Coulsdon are (foreground, left to right) Kenny Sansom, Vince Hilaire, Ian Evans, Peter Nicholas, Alan Leather, Alan Harris, Charlie Simpson and Terry Venables.

RIGHT: Kevin Keegan with Willie Wallace.

OVER, TOP LEFT: Watched by future World Cup Final referee Jack Taylor and Liverpool hardman Tommy Smith, Gerry Queen fires a shot past the lunging Larry Lloyd.

OVER, BOTTOM LEFT: John Toshack, Emlyn Hughes, Ross Jenkins and Peter Wall. Peter later broke his leg during this game, against his former teammates (see also page 68).

SHAKEN — NOT STIRRED

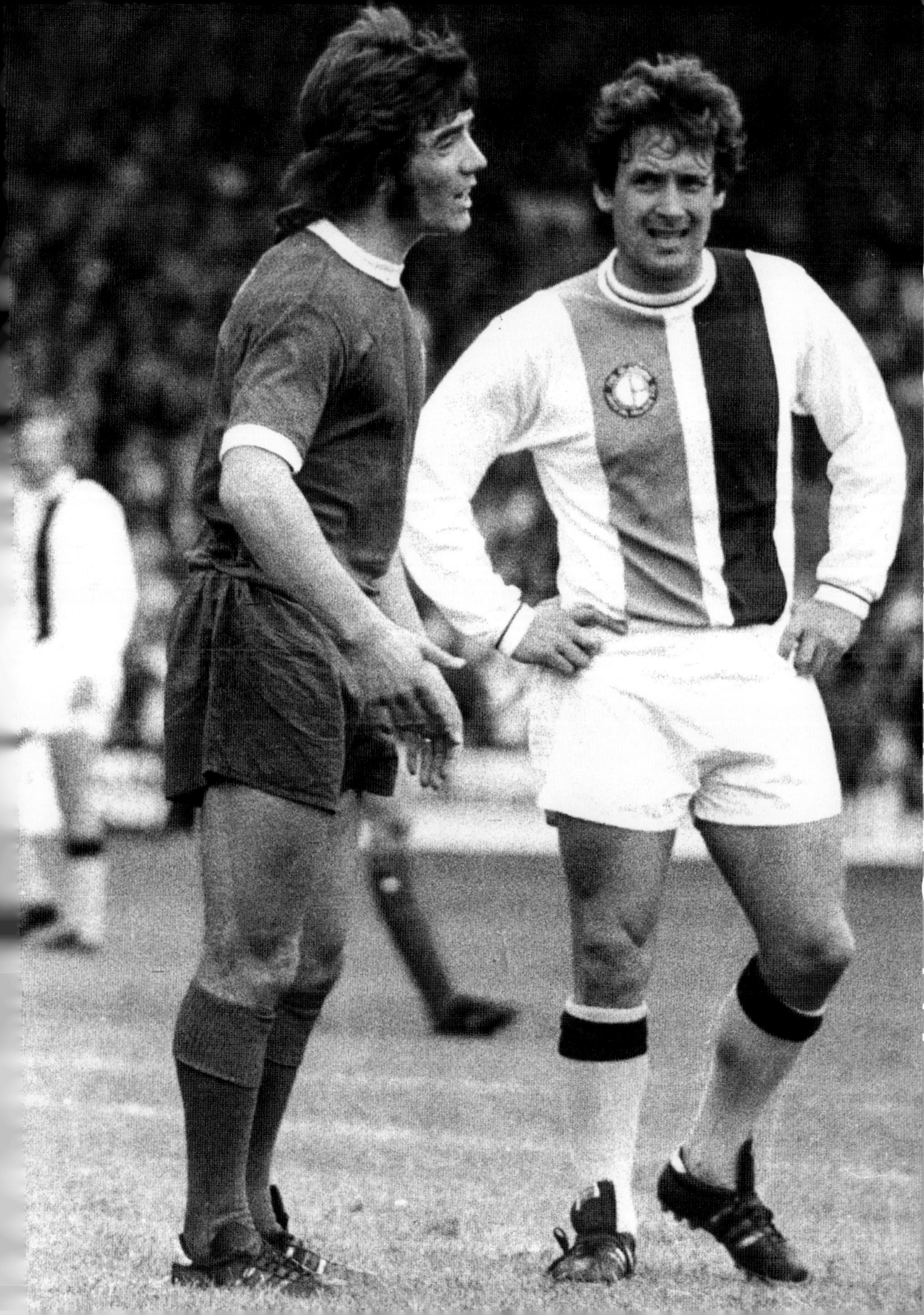

OPPOSITE PAGE, TOP RIGHT: Don Rogers celebrates his fantastic solo, debut goal against
Everton. In Hy's other shots from that game,
Iain Phillip rifles a shot in (with Alan Whittle,
who joined Palace less than 6 weeks later,
looking on) and in the main picture Rogers,
supported by David Payne (no.8) and Paddy
Mulligan, causes further concern to Everton.

 42

THIS PAGE: The 'Don' in all his majesty.

RIGHT: Giving them the slip at Anfield in front of over 50,000.

BELOW: Hurdling the Southampton 'keeper at Selhurst, then enjoying the roar of the fans after another stunning goal.

OPPOSITE, TOP: David Payne, a Palace stalwart with nine years as a professional at the Club comes up against another likely local lad, his former Palace skipper Steve Kember.

ALL OF THE TIME 72-73

BELOW: Hy captures Charlie Cooke twice, first against his former Chelsea teammates at Stamford Bridge, and then mesmerising England's Norman Hunter at Selhurst.

LEFT: John 'Yogi' Hughes skips over a challenge, while below he sneaks ahead of Don Rogers to fire in a shot past Norman Hunter (who is doing a fair impression of John Jackson).

ABOVE: Ex-Evertonian Alan Whittle 'gets the bird' at Anfield and decides his best option is to conduct the Kop in their witty ditties.

FAREWELL ARTHUR

Arthur Wait at his farewell party. Television commentator Brian Moore made the presentations. Wait had guided the club through all the divisions to reach the pinnacle of English football for the first time in their history.

Top Left: On the left is brother Bert Wait who served the Crystal Palace Supporters' Club.

Below Left: Wait emotionally takes the hand of long-serving Club Secretary Chris Hassell.

Above Sequence: Brian Moore takes the floor with Arthur's wife; Manager Head gives a speech; then shows Arthur a sample bust, similar to one planned to be sculpted of Arthur himself; to aid the sculptor, Hy took a series of reference portraits (far right).

Right: Arthur chatting with Bert. Could Arthur have co-existed with Malcolm Allison?

FAREWELL ARTHUR

49

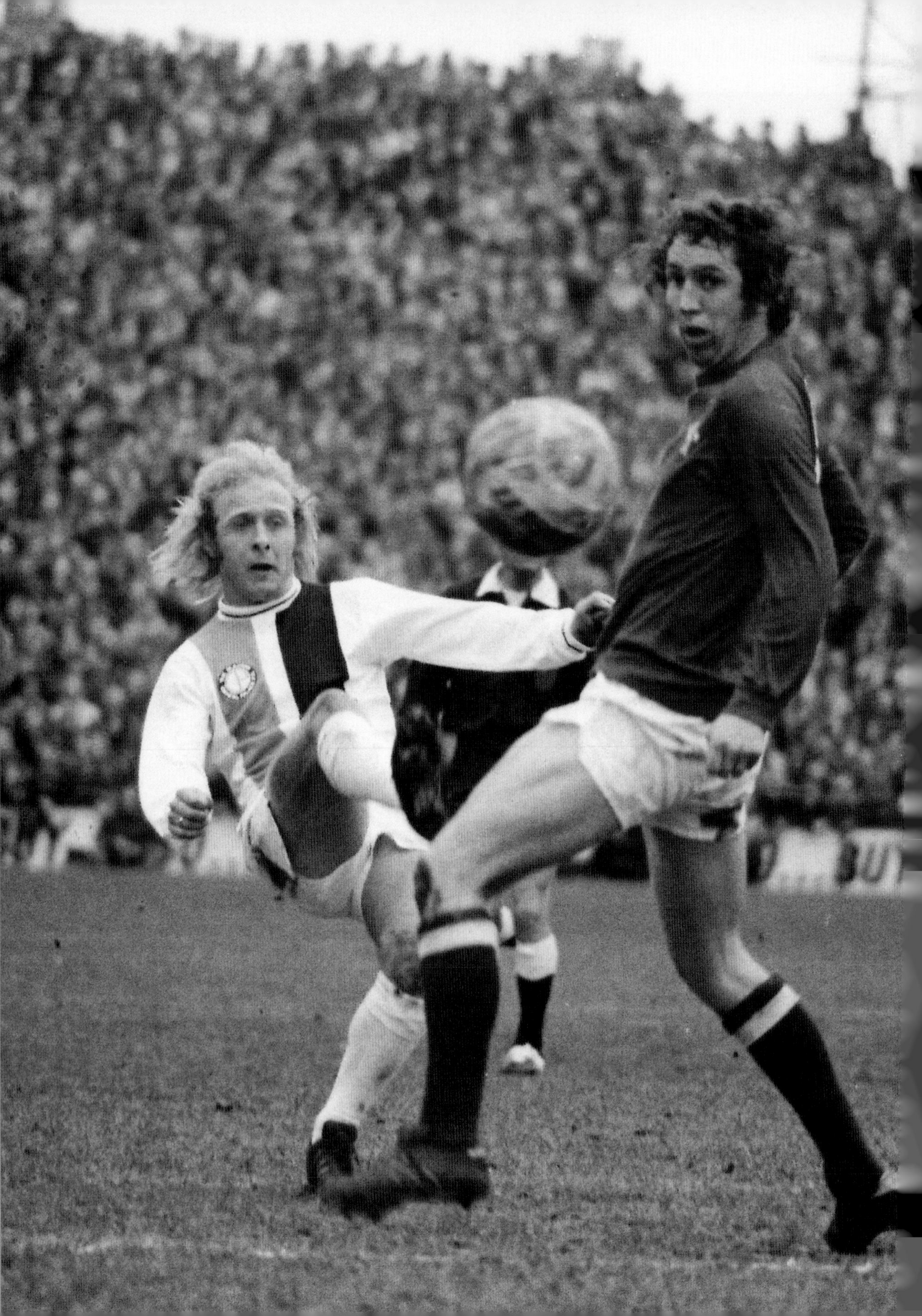

PREVIOUS PAGES: Alan Whittle sends a curling shot past Chelsea defender Marvin Hinton. Don Rogers has a Sheffield United defender mesmerised, and Bobby Kellard hangs on to the ball during a break in play, with David Payne and Iain Phillip in the background.

ABOVE AND CLOCKWISE: Don Rogers shoulder-to-shoulder with Tottenham's Ray Evans, Martin Hinshelwood fires in a shot against Stoke City, and Charlie Cooke, seemingly in splendid isolation, takes a free kick at the Holmesdale end.

RIGHT: Alan Whittle and Don Rogers leaving the field.

BELOW: Another Hy photo from the Spurs game, as Pat Jennings tips a cross over the bar watched by John Craven and Derek Possee of Palace, and Mike England, Ray Evans and Terry Naylor of Spurs.

ABOVE: March 31st, 1973, Malcolm Allison's first game in charge. Iain Phillip (number 4) has just put Palace ahead and is about to be embraced by fellow Scot, Tony Taylor. Derek Possee is no. 7.

BELOW: The Don avoids another slide rule challenge, and it's Chelsea's Hinton again.

RIGHT: Hello Hy. Malcolm Allison's surprise as he finds a lady photographer greeting his arrival at Selhurst.

ENTER BIG MAL

LEFT: Bert Head puts a brave face on the situation as he obligingly introduces new Manager Allison to the press.

BELOW: Assistant Manager Terry Long looks overcome with emotion as Mal's arrival spelt the beginning of the end to his eighteen year Palace career.

RIGHT: Tense moments as Malcolm is led into the dressing room to be introduced to the players for the first time. Through Hy's extraordinary, intimate photos one requires little imagination to sense the tension and hear the nervous laughter. Nail-chewers here include Jim Cannon, Iain Phillip and Don Rogers. Most at ease appear to be Bill Roffey (shaking Mal's hand, top left), Paddy Mulligan, and Charlie Cooke (second photo down, right). In contrast, John Jackson (top right, at the left) had every right to show concern. This series, showing a new Manager at the moment of introduction to his players, is quite unique in the history of sports photography.

ENTER BIG MAL

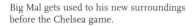

Big Mal gets used to his new surroundings before the Chelsea game.

BELOW: He acknowledges the cheers of the fans, who are positively bursting with anticipation. Bert Head (foreground) had accompanied him out onto the pitch.

CENTRE: Mal poses with his new Chairman, Ray Bloye, then signs autographs for Palace fans (note the rosette and, also, above the players' tunnel, the new Eagles crest. Palace were Glaziers no more).

FAR RIGHT: Jeff Johnson and Peter Taylor celebrate.

ENTER BIG MAL

Always be Mine 73-74

Hy Money's camera witnessed the demise of claret and blue shirts and Allison's introduction of red and blue stripes. Other innovative gimmicks introduced by Big Mal included numbers on sleeves and the Club Crest both dead-centre and occasionally on sleeves of shirts (left).

ABOVE: Dave 'Swindles' Swindlehurst, Peter Taylor and Alan Whittle.
LEFT: Derek Possee and Taylor again.
BELOW: 'Swindles' and 'Taff' Evans.
MIDDLE: Paul 'Doris' Hinshelwood and Swindlehurst.
FAR RIGHT, TOP: Rogers, Possee and Taylor.
FAR RIGHT, BOTTOM: Nicky Chatterton, after scoring against Charlton.

TO CAP IT ALL

MAIN PICTURE: Nine of Kenny Sansom's 87 full caps were won while still at the Palace.

INSET, LEFT ABOVE: Hy is present to capture the rare moment when no less than four Palace players line up in an England uniform, prior to the Under-23 game against Norway at The Dell in 1980. They are Terry Fenwick, Clive Allen, Vince Hilaire and Billy Gilbert.

INSET, LEFT BELOW: Ray Wilkins, later to be a Palace player (for all of 81 minutes) with Steve Coppell.

ABOVE: Terry Venables and England Manager Ron Greenwood.

IMMEDIATE LEFT: Peter Taylor at Selhurst prior to representing England Under-23s. Peter went on to become only the fourth Palace player to be capped by England as a full international.

BELOW: Kenny and Billy Gilbert on Under-23 duty in Oslo.

ABOVE: Proud dad Johnny Brooks with son Shaun. John made 7 appearances for the Palace at the tail end of his career. Shaun never equalled his father's achievement in playing for the full England team but he nevertheless made 66 appearances for Palace.

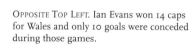

OPPOSITE TOP LEFT. Ian Evans won 14 caps for Wales and only 10 goals were conceded during those games.

LEFT: Peter Nicholas, Terry Boyle and Ian Walsh continued Palace's Welsh connection.

ABOVE: Steve Coppell can just be seen to the right of Peter Nicholas (4th in line) as the Wales and England sides come out at Wembley.

RIGHT: Jim Cannon and George Graham provide Palace's Scottish connection.

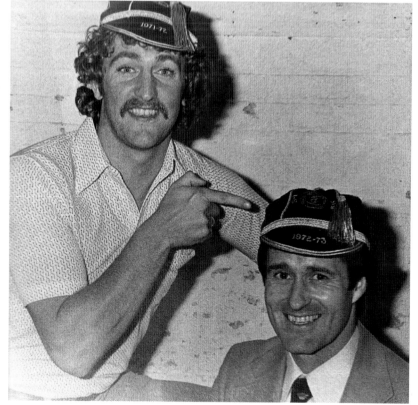

OUCH!

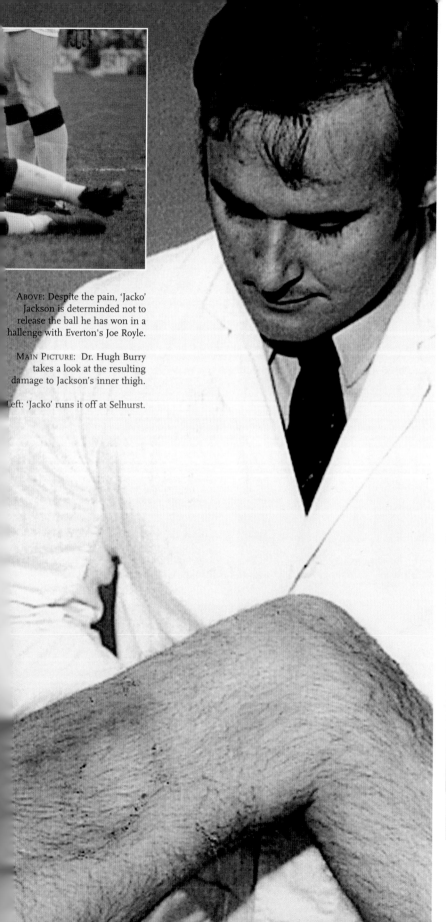

ABOVE: Despite the pain, 'Jacko'
Jackson is determined not to
release the ball he has won in a
challenge with Everton's Joe Royle.

MAIN PICTURE: Dr. Hugh Burry
takes a look at the resulting
damage to Jackson's inner thigh.

Left: 'Jacko' runs it off at Selhurst.

ABOVE AND BELOW: The tall, gangly young
striker Ross Jenkins is attended by the St.
John's Ambulance team.

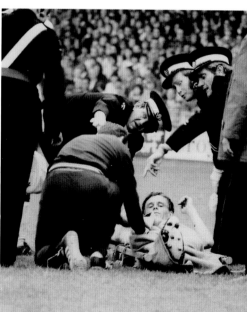

LEFT: Disaster strikes Peter Wall, leaving the field to discover later that his leg was broken.
ABOVE: Denis Law is treated at Selhurst. His Manchester United teammates here are Willie Morgan and Bobby Charlton. No. 4 for Palace is David Payne.
RIGHT: Jeff Johnson clutches his knee.
BELOW: Cooke watches Craven's treatment.
BELOW RIGHT: Ian Walsh against Spurs in '79 – only one sub allowed in those days!
ABOVE RIGHT: 'Swindles' being helped off by Dave Horn and Charlie Simpson.
RIGHT: Stan Ternent is among those helping carry Gary O'Reilly from the field.

Ian Evans breaks his leg against Fulham.

LEFT: Rachid Harkouk has to be restrained as Ian Evans lies flattened by a sickening tackle. It was immediately obvious that this was no ordinary injury by everyone who heard it. In effect, the double fracture to Ian's right leg ended a hugely promising career.

SEQUENCE BELOW: Hy captures Ian on crutches and when Ian finally made a comeback, against Leicester reserves.

OUCH!

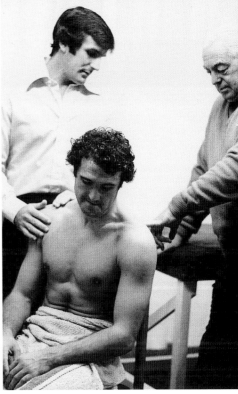

TOP LEFT: Kevin Mabbutt (Plaster of Palace?) just about makes it to this photo call... but only just.

LEFT: 'Satch' on stilts. Despite breaking his leg twice, Ian still managed to get two goals when coming on as substitute in the 1990 Cup Final.

ABOVE AND BELOW: John Burridge. Never a stranger to danger.

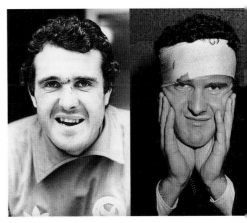

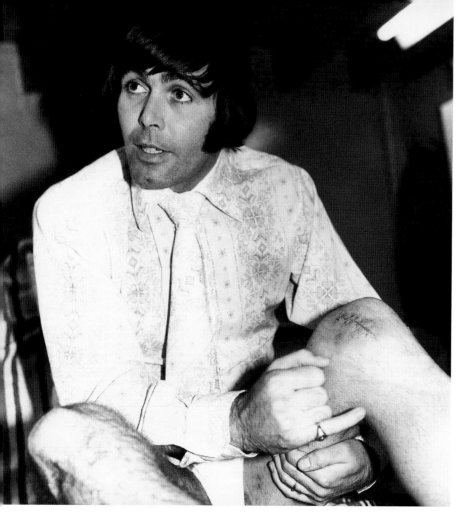

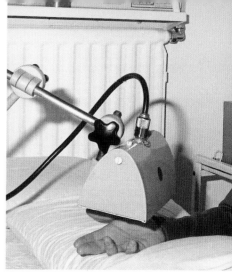

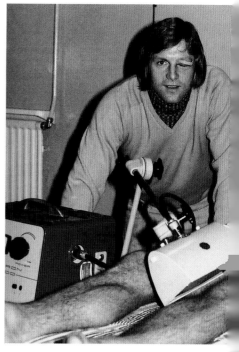

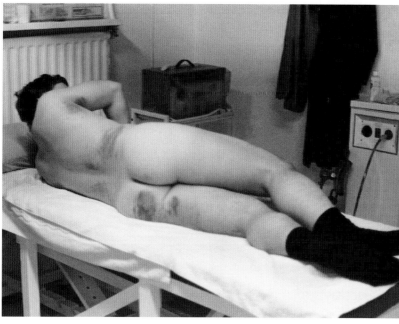

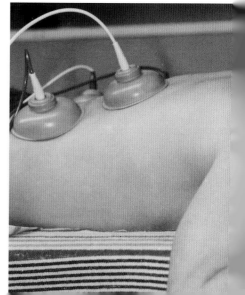

FAR LEFT, TOP: John 'Yogi' Hughes, injured against Sheffield United when he was the star of a 5-1 blunting of the Blades.

FAR LEFT, BOTTOM: Phil Holder suffers acid burns from sliding on pitch markings during a game at Vale Park, Port Vale.

CENTRE, TOP: Paul Hammond – happiness, is a warm hand.

CENTRE, MIDDLE: Yessir cap'n. Mel Blyth and Gerry Queen appear ready to audition for Peter Pan.

CENTRE, BOTTOM: 'Jacko' – abducted by aliens?

ABOVE: Former England captain Gerry Francis putting some weight on the foot.

RIGHT: Gerry again, with Peter Nicholas and Billy Gilbert – great feat.

Teammates bring a little light relief to Martin
Hinshelwood's recuperation programme. His
promising Palace career was beset by injury.
Opposite: Eyes on the ball. Dave Swindlehurst.

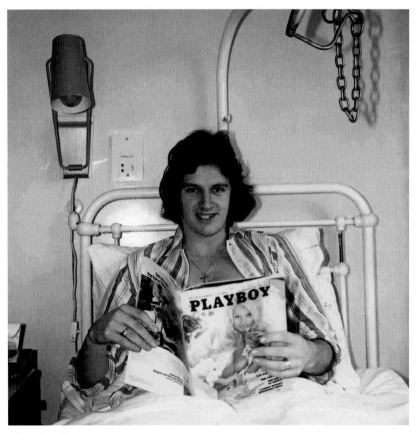

LEFT: Scorer Peter Taylor catches the exuberant Alan Whittle. Nick Chatterton and Dave Swindelhurst also enjoy the moment.

BELOW: A superb action shot from Hy. A haloed Jeff Johnson fires in a shot under the Selhurst lights.

RIGHT: Paddy Mulligan props up the post.

BOTTOM RIGHT: 'Swindles' skittles 'em over.

FAR LEFT: The diminutive Alan Whittle pleads for calm (probably from the referee).

ABOVE LEFT: Derek Possee scored 12 goals in 56 Palace appearances before joining former Palace coach George Petchey's Orient.

LEFT: Whittle had very quick feet. Hy captures him skipping between two floundering defenders.

ABOVE: As can be seen on these pages, at that time Palace possessed a number of players capable of destroying defences. Here Don Rogers skips past Phil Hoadley of Orient. Phil had been a product of the Selhurst youth set up and played 88 times for Palace before joining his former club captain John Sewell at the Orient, in September '71.

RIGHT: Jeff Johnson takes a quick breather.

THIS PAGE: Martin Hinshelwood shows his considerable tenacity, twice winning out against the same opponent. Peter Wall and Derek Jeffries look on (above).

OPPOSITE: Kenny Sansom does a 'Harry Worth'.

TOP LEFT AND CLOCKWISE: Bert Head casts a spell on Hy; "Gottle o' geer Gordon?" – Steve Coppell with the great Gordon Banks; Bassett, Hound of the Baskervilles; Vince Hilaire – the all round entertainer; Another fine mess, with Kenny Sansom an unconvincing Stan; finally, Terry puts Kenny's effort to shame.

THE LIGHTER SIDE

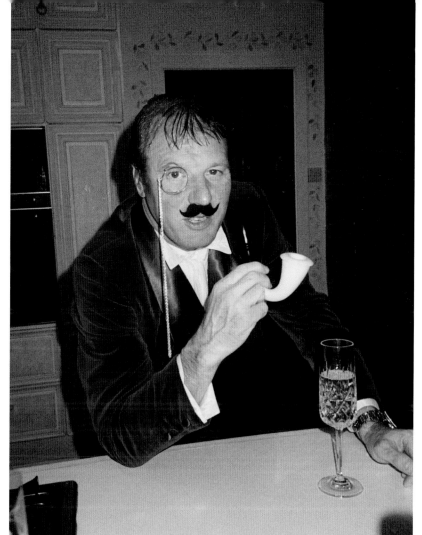
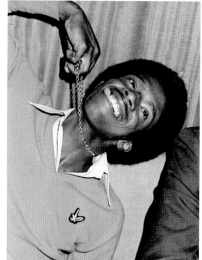
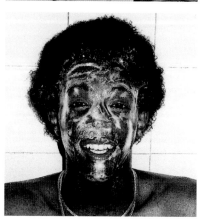

Ian Evans and Peter Taylor (above) and
Alan Whittle (below).

## BAD HAIR DAYS AND MISSING...

# ...BALLS

MISSING BALLS, CLOCKWISE FROM LEFT: Neil Smillie; Steve Perrin, Dave Swindlehurst and Southampton's Peter Osgood; Rachid Harkouk; Ian Walsh (with Terry Boyle, Gerry Francis, Mike Flanagan and Paul Hinshelwood); a training session with Ernie Walley.

SEQUENCE LEFT: Su Pollard of *Hi-De-Hi* (no, not *Hy-De-Hy*) fame is among a group of theatrical visitors to Selhurst; in such company Peter Taylor can't resist doing his famed Norman Wisdom impersonation before his shorts are unceremoniously pulled down.

THE LIGHTER SIDE

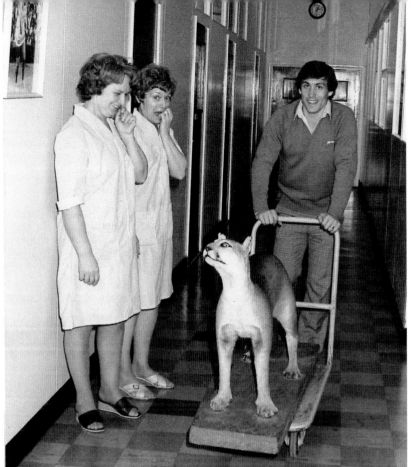

FURRY VISITORS, CLOCKWISE: Kenny brings along a (very tame) friend which has the Lynx effect on the ladies; 'Jacko' with Crystal the kitten; famed fan Chris Wright brings his best mate down for a trial on the wing. He's a good dribbler – geddit?

THE LIGHTER SIDE

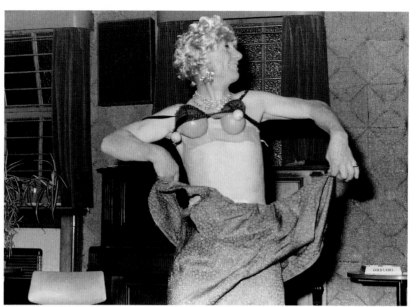

TO·DAYS M
POSTPO

CLOCKWISE FROM TOP LEFT: Len Chatterton
unveils in the Glaziers Club; Peter Nicholas –
"Your early morning call, sir – at the Main
Entrance"; Mike Elwiss and 'Budgie' – shar-
ing; mmmmwaa - Kenny Sansom takes a
fancy to no.6 and shocks the little blonde boy
in the front row AND the linesman; caring -
these opponents are a close-knit bunch; the
Selhurst Ski Resort opens as Kenny Sansom
gives Billy Gilbert a push but... where's the
slope?

Just Scratchin': John Burridge, Mel Blyth and Mick Hill.

Below: Peter nose best.

Opposite: Against Grimsby Town, 'Taff' Evans and Stewart Jump – jump!

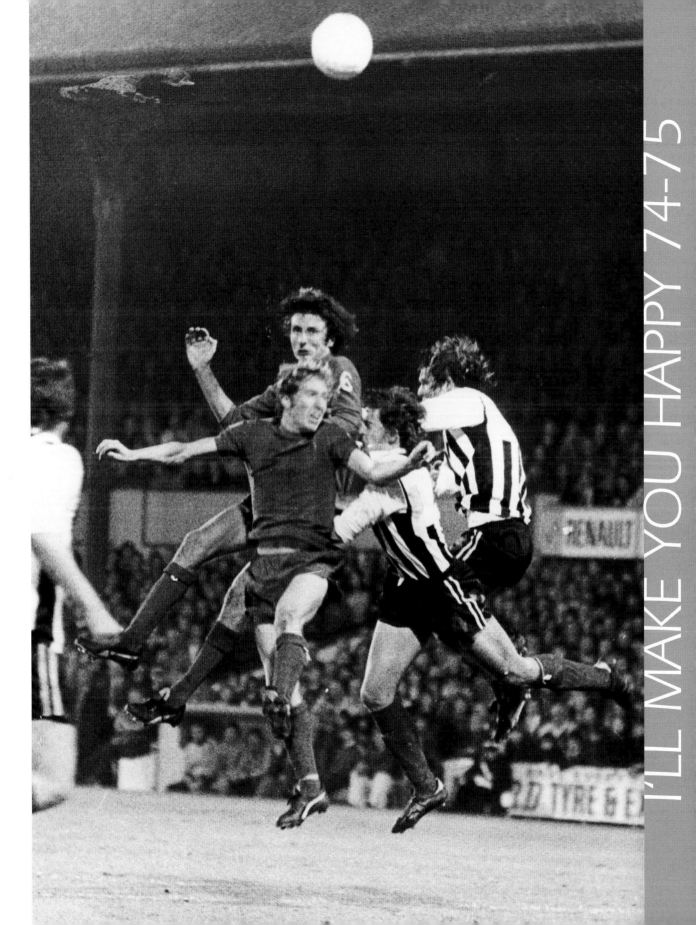

I'LL MAKE YOU HAPPY 74-75

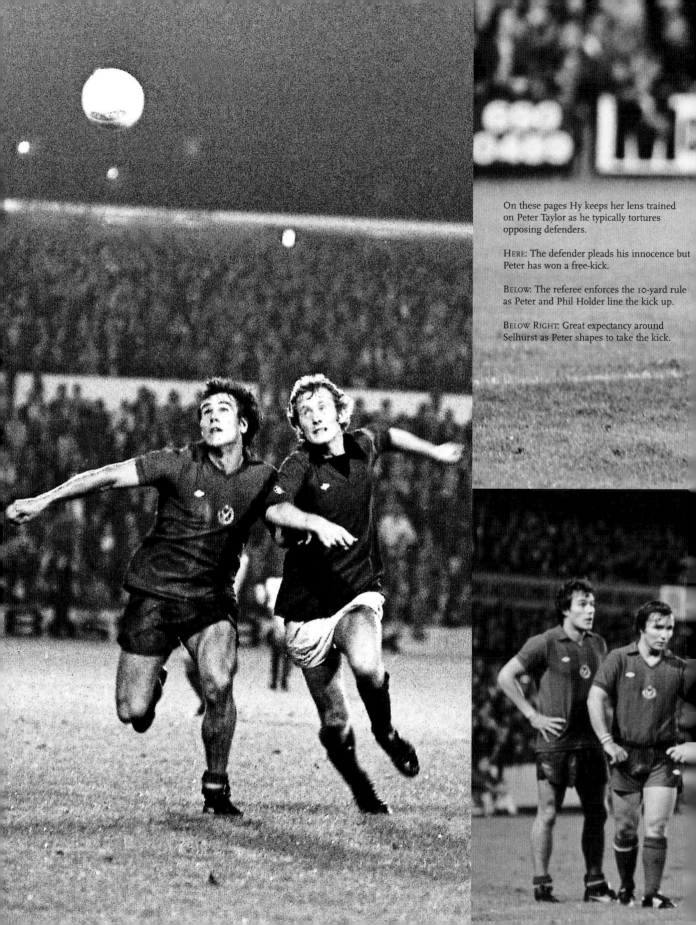

On these pages Hy keeps her lens trained on Peter Taylor as he typically tortures opposing defenders.

HERE: The defender pleads his innocence but Peter has won a free-kick.

BELOW: The referee enforces the 10-yard rule as Peter and Phil Holder line the kick up.

BELOW RIGHT: Great expectancy around Selhurst as Peter shapes to take the kick.

TOP LEFT: Peter Taylor comes up against Bobby Charlton, then Player-Manager at Preston.

LEFT: Hy's famous 'karate kick' photo of Taylor, playing against Millwall.

BELOW: In his third of only 14 appearances, Terry Venables tries to keep up with play!

ABOVE: Ian Evans – 'The General'…Flying High! By Hy.

TOP RIGHT: Phil Holder – drives to the by-line to get in a cross.

RIGHT: Holder again, preparing to take a throw-in.

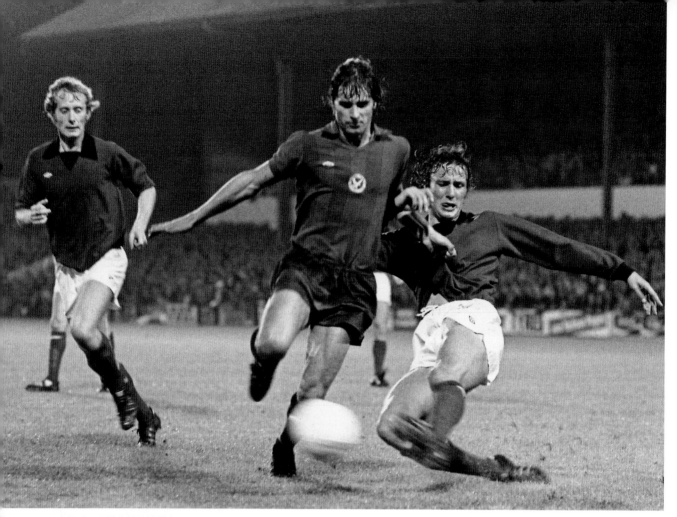

ABOVE: David Kemp scored a creditable 16 goals in 41 full appearances before going to Pompey in the deal that brought George Graham to Palace.

LEFT AND BELOW: A 3-0 defeat at Walsall on 25th April, 1975 ended Palace's chance of promotion.

RIGHT: The Eagles' perch, with the temporary Whitehorse Terrace in the foreground.

THE EAGLES' NEST

Hy Money takes a photographic interest in every aspect of the club, including its stadium. These three upper shots illustrate the division of the Holmesdale Road end (the 'Kop' at Selhurst) into three 'compounds'. Jim Cannon views the work at close hand.

BELOW: These merged photos of cricket taking place at Selhurst appear to shorten the Arthur Wait stand and give an idea of 'what might have been' for the devoted Holmesdale fans. The 'Palace Echo' with a roof over the immense terrace would surely have rivalled many others. Instead people began to stay away with crowds slipping below the 5,000 mark. Cricket was one possible new revenue stream. However, as can be seen below, Cricket wasn't going to be the answer.

LEFT: Len Chatterton in pitchside discussions.
ABOVE: The Whitehorse 'corner' joined seamlessly with the Arthur Wait enclosure. With a full ground, the view of the action offered shows what a well thought-out plan for the stadium Wait's had been. Note disabled cars at the top of the terracing.
BELOW: Hy caught everyone sneaking out.

RIGHT: The Whitehorse / Park Road junction – Away Day in '76. The Whitehorse was an exceptional 'Away' end with many home devotees. These corner angles show how well 'the wall' end worked alongside the Arthur Wait stand. Indeed the original proclamation by AJ was to make Selhurst 'the Highbury of South London'.

BELOW: This view shows that it had the potential to be truly gargantuan, possibly bigger even than the Holte End at Villa Park. Already, the financial and physical cracks were starting to appear though (centre-right).

THE EAGLES' NEST

The vertical sequence of Hy's shots on the far left show the coarse ground of the old brickyard – now Sainsburys' car park (from top to bottom): from the terrace... Lady Edridge School on the left and the Social Hall and the ball courts. This is followed by three other views taken from the car park. The lower two shots show the considerable expanse behind the Whitehorse Lane end.

SEQUENCE NEAR LEFT: During construction, football continued at Selhurst – but not as we'd known it. Here the various stages of development show the monstrosity under construction. Within five years, nearly a quarter of a century of prudent growth and hard work had been wiped out in a land deal that had to be investigated by the Inland Revenue.

RIGHT: For a while the original terracing remained.

ABOVE: It was later replaced by a workable terrace since covered by seats.

The Main Stand at Selhurst Park, designed by Archibald Leitch, was opened in 1924. Various, largely cosmetic changes have been made to it over the years, but the structure is still intrinsically the same as when first built.

TOP LEFT: Jim Cannon outside the Glaziers entrance. The Main Entrance is under the overhanging Vice Presidents and Board Room, as it is still today.

BOTTOM LEFT: This matchday crowd scene is the view from the extension seen in the upper photo. Lady Edridge School, to the right of the fence, is now the location of flats.

MIDDLE LEFT: The stairwell indicating the ground-breaking(!) idea of ground-sharing.

THIS PAGE: The enclosure makes way for a completely seated Main Stand. It certainly made it more difficult to abuse the directors, although on occasion they were the only ones there.

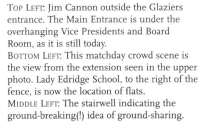

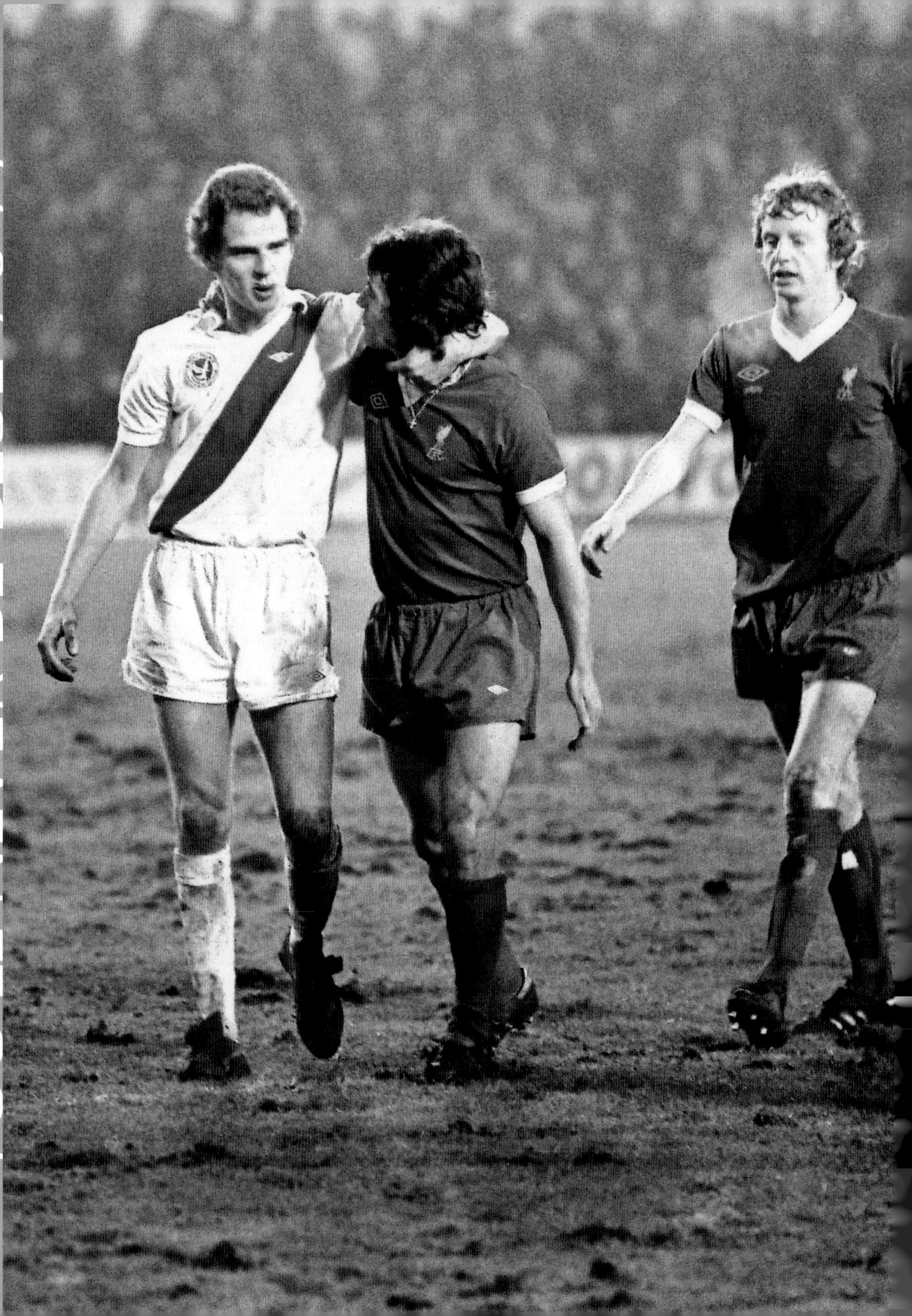

PAGES 106-110: In season 1937-38 Palace drew 0-0 with Liverpool in the F.A. Cup 3rd Round. 39 years to the day, the teams met at Anfield and the score once again was 0-0. The game at Anfield and the replay acted as a marker to the wider football world that Palace were on their way back.

LEFT: Leaving the field, Paul Hinshelwood is congratulated by Kevin Keegan with 'Super-Sub' David Fairclough following.

ABOVE: England's Ray Clemence wonders what a balloon is doing at a football match.

RIGHT AND BELOW: George Graham was every-where at Anfield – here seen with Nicky Chatterton and (below) Barry Silkman.

FACING PAGE, TOP: At Anfield Nicky Chatterton is pictured both in aerial combat (with Phil Holder and Emlyn Hughes looking on) and alone, gritting his teeth.
FACING PAGE, BOTTOM: Graham leaps with Hughes, Holder again in the background.

ABOVE: 'Fish' Hinshelwood lets one fly with a corker to score for Palace at Selhurst.
RIGHT: Graham and Hughes again.
BELOW: Dave Swindlehurst evades Heighway's challenge and (bottom) Steve Perrin dives to get a header on target.

TOP LEFT: Graham beats Phil Thompson.
ABOVE: A study in concentration. Dave Swindlehurst and Emlyn Hughes.
BELOW: Heighway, Hinshelwood and Perrin.
LEFT: Two great opponents, Kevin Keegan and Kenny Sansom. Game over, and it is back to the League for Palace.

YOU'LL NEVER BE BLUE 76-77

Palace finished season 76-77 by pulling in 13 points from the last 8 games. Hy captures some of the stalwarts of that season.

ABOVE: Phil Holder shoots.

TOP RIGHT: Calcutta-born Ricky Heppolette is involved in a four-footed challenge.

BELOW: Stewart Jump starred in 91 games before going to play in the States.

RIGHT: Ian Evans outjumps Jim Cannon.

ON THE ROAD

LEFT: Does Vince really look like he's on the phone – it's a pretty big aerial! Kenny Sansom must be thinking the same thing.

ABOVE: Steve Kember takes up 'coaching' duties with Jerry 'Smurf' Murphy.

RIGHT: Paul 'Doris'/'Fish' Hinshelwood was converted from forward to right back by Venables, and was always good coming forward from the back.

BELOW: Ian Walsh, superstar. This car would get attention in the Valleys even now.

Top Left. Tony Taylor never ran out of gas on the field.

Left: Fitting Ian Evans into a Mini is about the best promotion the car could get.

Bottom Left: Stretching off to Cardiff for the 2004 Play-Off Final.

Below: Ken and Vince again.

ABOVE: John Burridge, Peter Nicholas and Jim Cannon come up for air.

RIGHT: Jim with the new model.

BOTTOM RIGHT: A.J. Wait was a trendsetter with his personalised number plates.

ABOVE: Now *that's* a car. Pure genius, with Len Chatterton at the wheel. Nookie explains to Roger deCourcey what's going on. The 'Flatterer' was a converted old Fiat 127. Still with full number plates and tax disc.

BELOW, MIDDLE: Terry Fenwick and pals.

BOTTOM: Billy Gilbert – it's a bit James Bond isn't it, Billy? Not a patch on Len's.

RIGHT: Receptionist Lyn Wattis greets Mr. Donald Rogers on his first day.

SIGN ON. . . .

Changing of the Guard.

ABOVE: Paddy Mulligan and Charlie Cooke both arrived from Chelsea in September, 1972.

RIGHT, ABOVE AND BELOW: 30th October, 1972. Don Rogers teams up with former Swindon Manager Head, and takes the field against Everton, to great expectation from the crowd, even the milkman.

BELOW: Don was soon joined by Alan 'We Want' Whittle (here greeted by Mel Blyth), captured from Everton on 9th December and ready for his heady debut against The Red Devils at Selhurst Park.

ABOVE: New boy Derek Possee arrived in January, 1973, and is introduced to his new teammates by Terry Long. They include (l-r): 'Jacko' Jackson, Tony Taylor, Don Rogers, Charlie Cooke, Iain Phillip and Alan Whittle.

BELOW: A left hand shake for Clive Allen who came from Arsenal with goalkeeper Paul Barron, in the disastrous swap deal that saw Kenny Sansom fly the nest. This ultimately led to the collapse of the whole deck of cards. Venables himself left for QPR on the 30th of October with Palace rooted to the bottom of the table.

BORED ROOM

Forty-one years of the Crystal Palace story have been shaped by these two gentlemen. To your left, 'Uncle' Ron Noades and (this page), erm, 'Uncle' Arthur Wait, seen at home (below) with the original Mel B. and (above) solving a jigsaw puzzle.

ABOVE: Raymond Bloye's seven years in charge as Chairman bring mixed emotions, but exemplify what makes supporting Crystal Palace 'interesting'.

BELOW: Bloye at Selhurst with Ian Smith, the President of Rhodesia, who pushed for major-ity rule for what later became Zimbabwe.

RIGHT, TOP: Arriving for Burnley '79 with, among others, John Bailey of the Vice President's Club (glasses, to the rear).

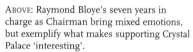

CESSORIES FOR

LEFT, MIDDLE: England's World Cup Winning Manager, Sir Alf Ramsey, squeezes between Bert Head and Ray Bloye.

BOTTOM LEFT: King Olaf of Norway.

ABOVE: Ray Bloye spots Hy as she takes this

shot of her sons Stuart and Martin meeting up with Malcolm Allison.

BELOW: Getting the hair right. Terry Venables and Ray Bloye with Palace directors.

ABOVE: Ron finally found his Prince for the Palace in a young Steve Coppell. Over the years their formidable partnership led to Palace's most successful era ever. Due to iron-disciplined prudence, the green shoots of

THIS PAGE, TOP TO BOTTOM: Ron Noades on his very first day in charge; studying Hy's pictures in the 80/81 Year Book; a rare 'hirsute' Ron; and finally, is that Richard Gere or Nick 'The Scoop' Harling?

BORED ROOM

recovery finally flowered in a cauldron of
emotion against Blackburn in the Play Off
Final (below).
RIGHT: Chairman of the Bored with Sam
Hammam and Gino Santin.

BORED ROOM

ABOVE: Malcolm's last stand.

RIGHT AND BELOW: Novello Noades epitomises the changing climate in the once 'stuffy' boardroom, as further witnessed with this group of Director's wives in their bubbly covey hole.

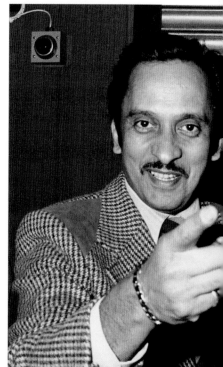

Upper Left: Bobby Moore with Tel.

Left, Middle: Life-President Stanley Stephenson (with hat) sits behind England Manager Ron Greenwood.

Left, Bottom: Agi/Agi/Agi DeSouza, VP who nearly took over the Club on one occasion, with a Daily Mirror reporter.

Above: Peter Morley – founder VP member and Chairman of the Trust.

Below: Club Secretary Alan Leather once worked with Jimmy Hill at Coventry City. Brian Moore is to the right.

Next Page: Simon Jordan.

FAR RIGHT: Camp it up lads! Rogers and Whittle.

A WORLD OF RED N'BLUE. CLOCKWISE FROM TOP LEFT: Coach 2, 1976; Luke's card display, Palace v.Southampton, May 2005; the Eagles have landed;the Palace flag; Norwegian fans at Blackburn; Hy wrecks the dug-out.

PREVIOUS PAGE: Maurice Drewitt ushers in the modern era, proudly showing off the fans' new paint job.

LEFT AND ABOVE: Unusual team-group photographs by Hy, from different eras, including a little bare-faced cheek!

SEQUENCE, TOP AND RIGHT: Action from the thrilling second leg of the Play-Off Final against Blackburn, including Ian Wright tucking the opening goal away from Alan Pardew's outside-of-the-foot cross.

ABOVE: Dave Madden's penalty is scooped out of the net by Gary O'Reilly. At 3-3, Palace were now ahead on away goals. Dave 'The Mod' reels away in unforgettable celebratory style.
BELOW: The Directors toast Palace's 'Bouncebackability' after the victory.

THE FOLLOWING ELEVEN PAGES CELEBRATE THE F.A. CUP FINAL, 12/5/90:

The biggest day in the history of Crystal Palace Football Club, and, of course, Hy was there.

TOP LEFT: Sir Stanley Stephenson on the way to Wembley.

TOP RIGHT: Palace fans make their mark.

CENTRE: A proud and solitary Steve Coppell.

BELOW LEFT: Top head gear.

BELOW RIGHT: Two players' wives dressed for the occasion.

# Suits you, Sir!

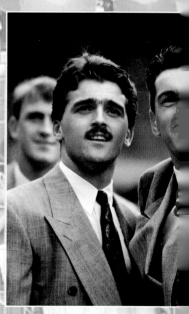

On these pages Hy captures just how competitive and thrilling the 1990 Final was.

OVERLEAF: 'Satchmo' the great! Ian scores Palace's 2nd and 3rd goals and says a little thank you.

AUDIO
VIDEO

ACE    3
UTD.   2

8

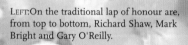

LEFT: On the traditional lap of honour are, from top to bottom, Richard Shaw, Mark Bright and Gary O'Reilly.

ABOVE: Come back soon. We did.

BELOW: Ron and Novello Noades.

BELOW: Special guest Big Mal.

ABOVE: The Cup Final cake.

RIGHT, TOP TO BOTTOM: The Burtons' suits get another airing at the evening reception.

In the Cup Final replay Palace's choice of strip was as disappointing as the result, United winning 1-0. Here Phil Barber and Richard Shaw gang up on United's Webb.
ABOVE: Andy Thorn, Nigel Martyn and Geoff Thomas lead a somewhat disconsolate lap of honour.
BELOW: Heroes one and all.

THE FEDORA CUP RUN

F.A. Cup 4th Round, 1976. Leeds United didn't lose often at home and few teams went there with any true confidence, but 3rd Division Palace did.

THIS PAGE: Three pictures showing the goal from Peter Taylor's free kick, converted by David 'Goliath' Swindlehurst.

LEFT: The anxious Leeds wall, made up of Lorimer, Yorath and Bremner, await Peter Taylor's free-kick.

MAIN PICTURE: Swindlehurst cuts behind England's Madeley and heads past Harvey.

RIGHT: Ian Evans hugs Taylor, the provider.

146

TOP LEFT: Alan Whittle goes into the referee's book.

TOP RIGHT: At the final whistle, Whittle shakes Madeley's hand as the referee calls for the game ball from goalkeeper Harvey.

ABOVE: Swindlehurst leaps again, with another England player, Cherry, as Nick Chatterton bursts through the middle watched by Scotland's Bremner.

MIDDLE RIGHT: Terry on the touchline.

RIGHT: Jim Cannon with the headlines he had helped create. Powerful Leeds humbled by lowly Palace!

5th Round. Away again, this time to Chelsea.
FAR LEFT, TOP: Peter Taylor fires into the far corner from Nick Chatterton's lay-off. 1-0!
MIDDLE, ABOVE: Alan Whittle follows up

Taylor's second and winning goal, direct from a free kick.
ABOVE: Despondent Chelsea after the goal.
OPPOSITE, BOTTOM: Ian Evans brushes off

Garner to brilliantly flick a header at goal.
BELOW: Hy's superb shot of Alan Whittle unleashing a rocket past lunging Micky Droy.

ABOVE: Super Jim Cannon flies through the air with the greatest of ease, putting Ian Evans at some risk.

RIGHT: At the final whistle 'Swindles' and Terry embrace.

The 54,407 attendance at Stamford Bridge was only 1,770 short of Palace's biggest ever. The sash kit was worn for the first time here at Chelsea and was to become one of the most popular and enduring of Palace uniforms over the coming years.

There was a down side to the Cup run – Palace won just six out of their last twenty-six League games.

6th March 1976. F.A. Cup, 6th Round, Quarter Final stage. Sunderland 0 Crystal Palace 1, played before another 50,850 (including 2,000+ Palace fans who arrived late!).
LEFT: 'The' hat cuts a dash amidst the flat

caps. Mal and Ray Bloye look relaxed.
ABOVE: Dave Swindlehurst appears to spot Hy among a sea of legs.
RIGHT: Nick Chatterton chases a through ball.
BELOW: 'Swindles' in two great action poses.

ABOVE: A great sequence from Hy as Peter Taylor's speed leaves a Sunderland defender struggling in his wake - clearly the end result was hardly what Peter wanted!

BELOW: Sunderland captain Moncur heads clear against a wallpaper of standing fans.
RIGHT: Another wonderful Hy photo of Sunderland's 'Torturer-in-Chief'.

PREVIOUS SPREAD: Superb work by Hy once again, capturing the very moment as Whittle pirouettes between Jeff Clarke and Dick Malone to slam home for 'one of the sweetest goals I have ever scored'.

ABOVE: Alan Whittle accepts the plaudits coming from the Director's Box.

ABOVE, CENTRE: Who let that lady into the dressing rooms? Jim Cannon and Martin Hinshelwood seem pleased to see Hy. A poignant picture, as this would prove to be the highlight of Martin's Palace career. Only three days later he was to suffer a cartilage injury against Port Vale that ended his career despite many brave comebacks.

LEFT: Hero of the hour Whittle.

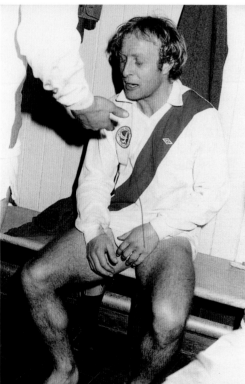

THE FEDORA CUP RUN

ABOVE: In Sunderland Wonderland are (standing) Martin, Jim, Phil, Paul, Nicky and Alan; (seated) Terry, Peter, Dave, Peter, Derek and Malcolm; (on the deck) Dave Horn, Ian and Charlie Simpson.

LEFT: Peter Wall – 'man of the match' – celebrates in true 70's style – he accepts a fag from Alan Whittle!

RIGHT: As Crystal Palace A.F.C. reached their first domestic Cup Semi-Final, so a crop of school kids were doing the same in the F.A. Youth Cup. Ready to board the train, Terry was to mould those kids into the team he took to Division One in 1979.

The journey home.

Above: Big Mal gets a soaking from an over-exhuberant Chris Wright.

Below: The Palace directors catch their coach connection to the station.

Right: As was the way with the away travel then, the team shared the train with returning fans. Hy was on hand to capture the party mood in this series of shots from the trip.

Following Spread: More celebrations on the train. Kenny shares the journey on his proud mum's lap with Steve Perrin on the right of the picture. Alan Whittle dons the ticket inspector's hat. Maurice Drewitt and Chris Wright are on hand to patch up a brick-shattered window.

THE FEDORA CUP RUN

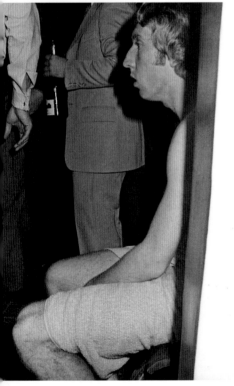

From joy...to pain. The Semi-Final. After Palace's success away to Leeds, Chelsea and Sunderland it was Second Division Southampton who entered this game as 'underdogs'.

SEQUENCE ABOVE: (far left and far right) Alan Harris and Terry Venables do their utmost to hide the disappointment. The same can't be said for Paul Hammond and Jim Cannon (centre).

BOTTOM LEFT: Stewart Jump appears to be in shock.

BELOW: T.V. commentator Brian Moore enters the dressing room to interview grim-faced

THE FEDORA CUP RUN

Derek Jeffries and Ian Evans. The contrasting public and private faces show the realisation from the players of how close Palace had been to be the first team from Division 3 to reach the Cup Final. Malcolm Allison had maintained all season that Palace would be promoted AND win the FA Cup! Following the failure to win promotion he convinced the board that Terry was the man for his job. Just a year later, at a Selhurst Park reserve game and amongst a small pocket of fans at the Racecourse Ground in Wales, the pain was to turn into unbridled joy.

# BACK ON THE UP

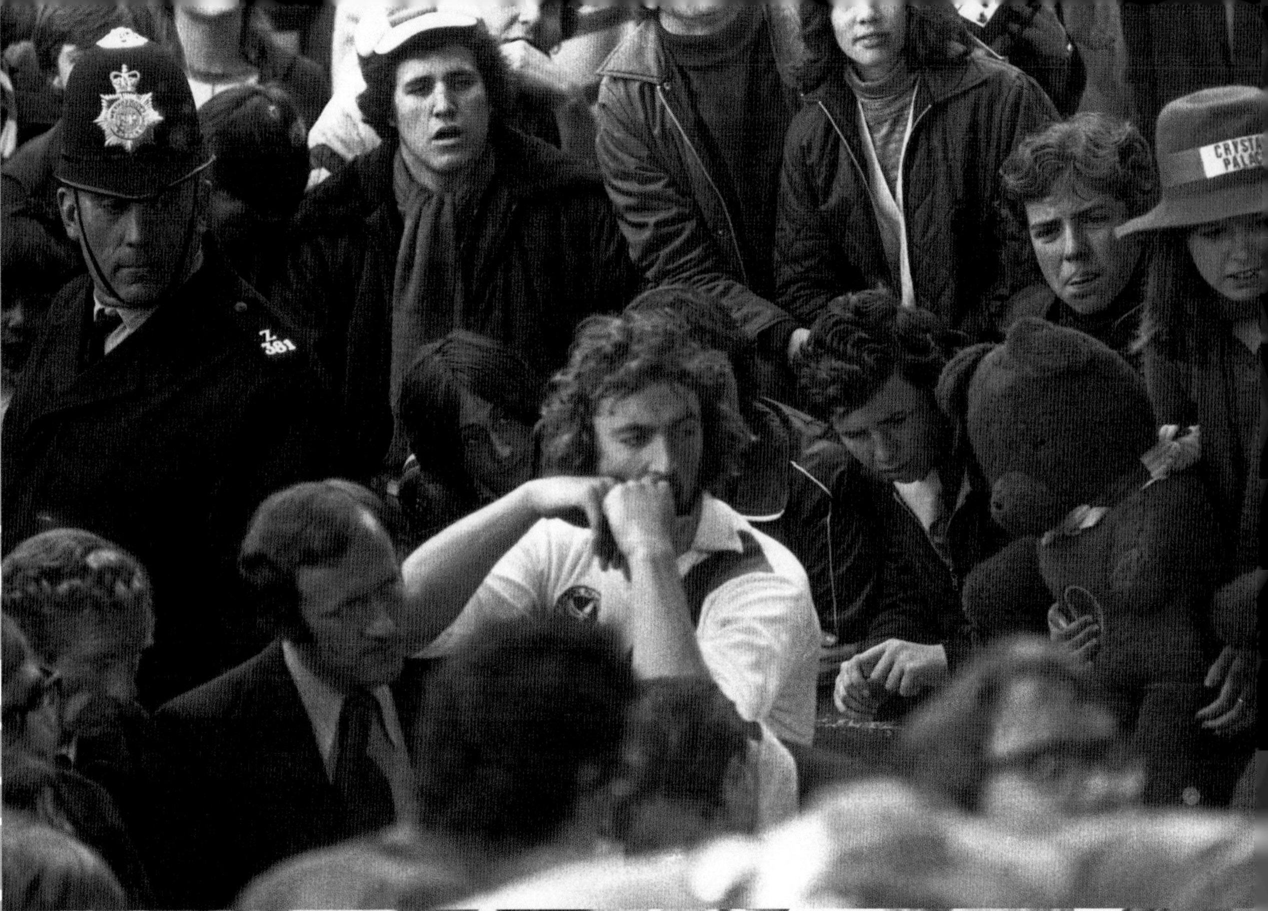


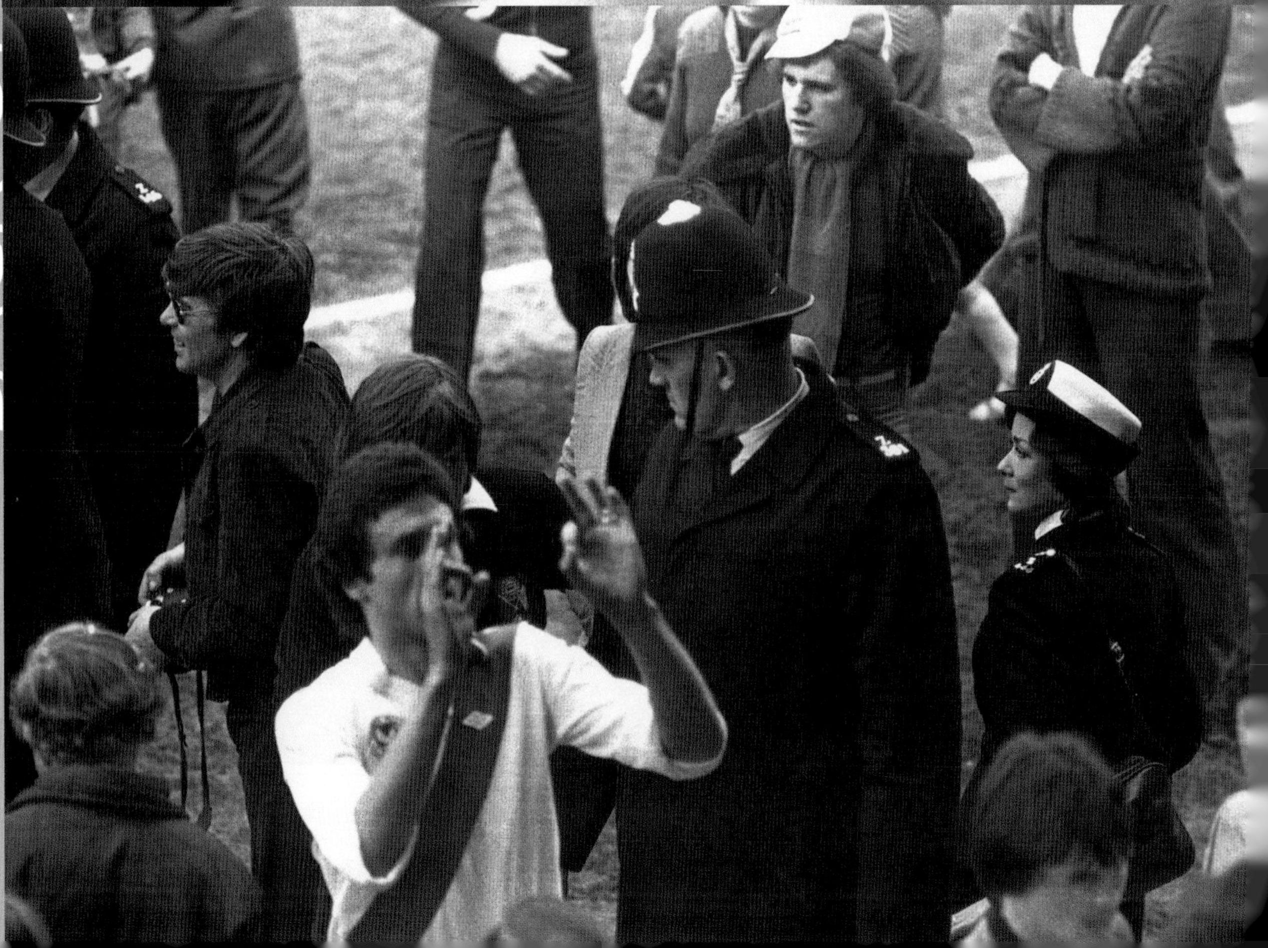

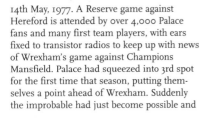

14th May, 1977. A Reserve game against Hereford is attended by over 4,000 Palace fans and many first team players, with ears fixed to transistor radios to keep up with news of Wrexham's game against Champions Mansfield. Palace had squeezed into 3rd spot for the first time that season, putting themselves a point ahead of Wrexham. Suddenly the improbable had just become possible and Wrexham had to beat Mansfield to pip us. PREVIOUS PAGES: Ian Evans signals anxiously that the Racecourse score is still 0-0. Then news comes through that Wrexham have lost 1-0. The first souvenir to be strewn into the crowd is Chairman Ray Bloye's hat, followed later by player's apparel. Crystal Palace were back on the up.

Opposite and Below: Rachid Harkouk, Dave
Swindlehurst and (below) Barry Silkman
acknowledge the fans at Selhurst.

Above: Hy is in the Director's Box to catch
this atmospheric close-up of the hatless Bloye.

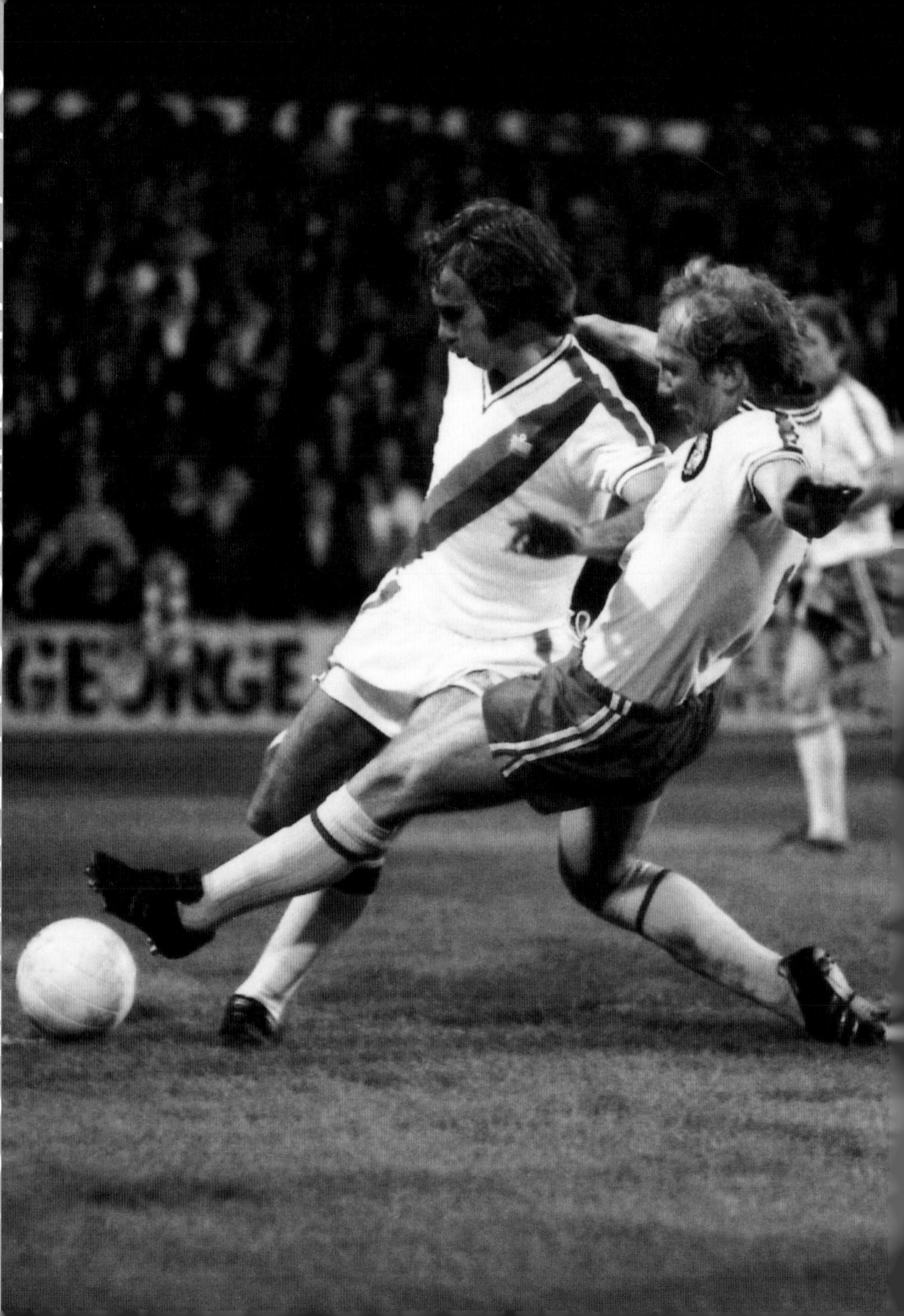

OPPOSITE PAGE: The 'sash' kit Malcolm Allison had adapted from Manchester City's Red and Black for the Chelsea Cup game was now established and for the new season received a modern update. Here, Jeff Bourne gets in a shot against Southampton. The previous season he came in for the last 15 games of the promotion push and scored 9 goals.

THIS PAGE: Three of Hy's action shots from Palace's 2-2 draw with Tottenham at White Hart Lane.

ABOVE: Peter Nicholas and Paul Hinshelwood combine to clear under pressure from John Duncan and Colin Lee. The Palace 'keeper is Tony Burns.

LEFT: Phil Holder performing in front of the fans where he began his career.

BELOW: Great action captured superbly by Hy again, as Duncan dives ahead of Jim Cannon to acrobatically head at goal.

TOP LEFT: Panoramic view as 'Jimbo' and a Bolton opponent lay spreadeagled. Sam Allardyce towers over the resulting melée. Palace players are (l-r) Evans, Chatterton, Hilaire, Bourne, Graham, and Harkouk.
FAR LEFT: Watched by Dave Swindlehurst, Paul Hinshelwood and Bolton's Ian Morgan, Jim Cannon pokes the ball past the onrushing 'keeper. Unfortunately the referee also watches, with whistle to his mouth.
LEFT: Kenny Sansom also one-on-one.
ABOVE: Nick Chatterton hustling.
BELOW: Kenny receives the ball in readiness for one of his long throws.

ABOVE AND BELOW: 'Swindles' in typically spectacular action, photographed typically spectacularly by Hy.

LEFT: *Two* hands, Billy!
OPPOSITE: Mounted Police in Park Road for the visit of Brighton.

EVENIN' ALL

ABOVE AND CLOCKWISE: Ron helps Police with their enquiries. Beryl hoping for a pull, as Len gets a ticket. Blowing the whistle. "Careful how you tell him what to do with it, Terry". Pompey fans fill the Holmesdale, 1987. Aaah, the days of Punks and Skins. Segregation at the Whitehorse end. Using the latest palm-held camcorders (centre).

# I'LL ALWAYS BE TRUE 78-79

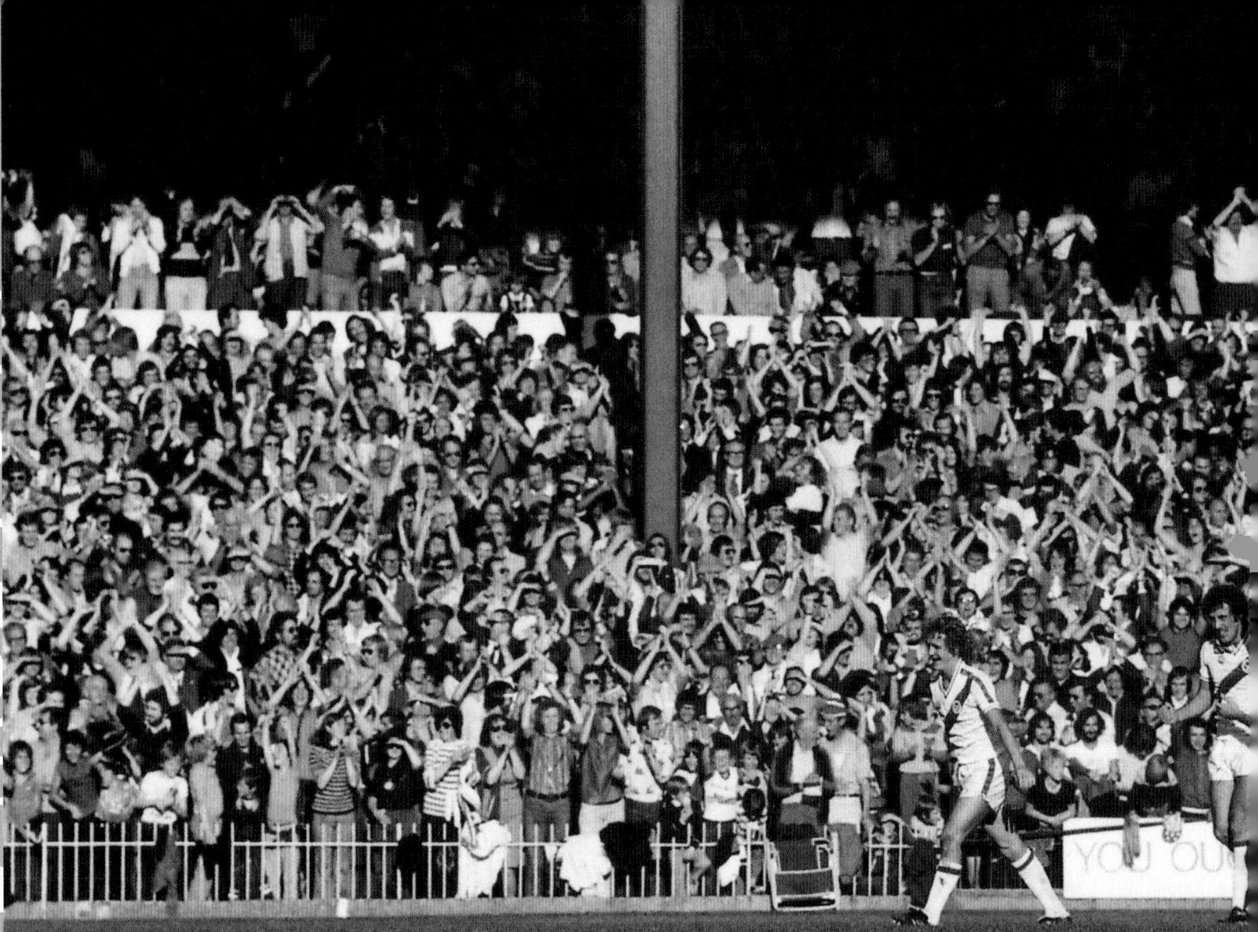

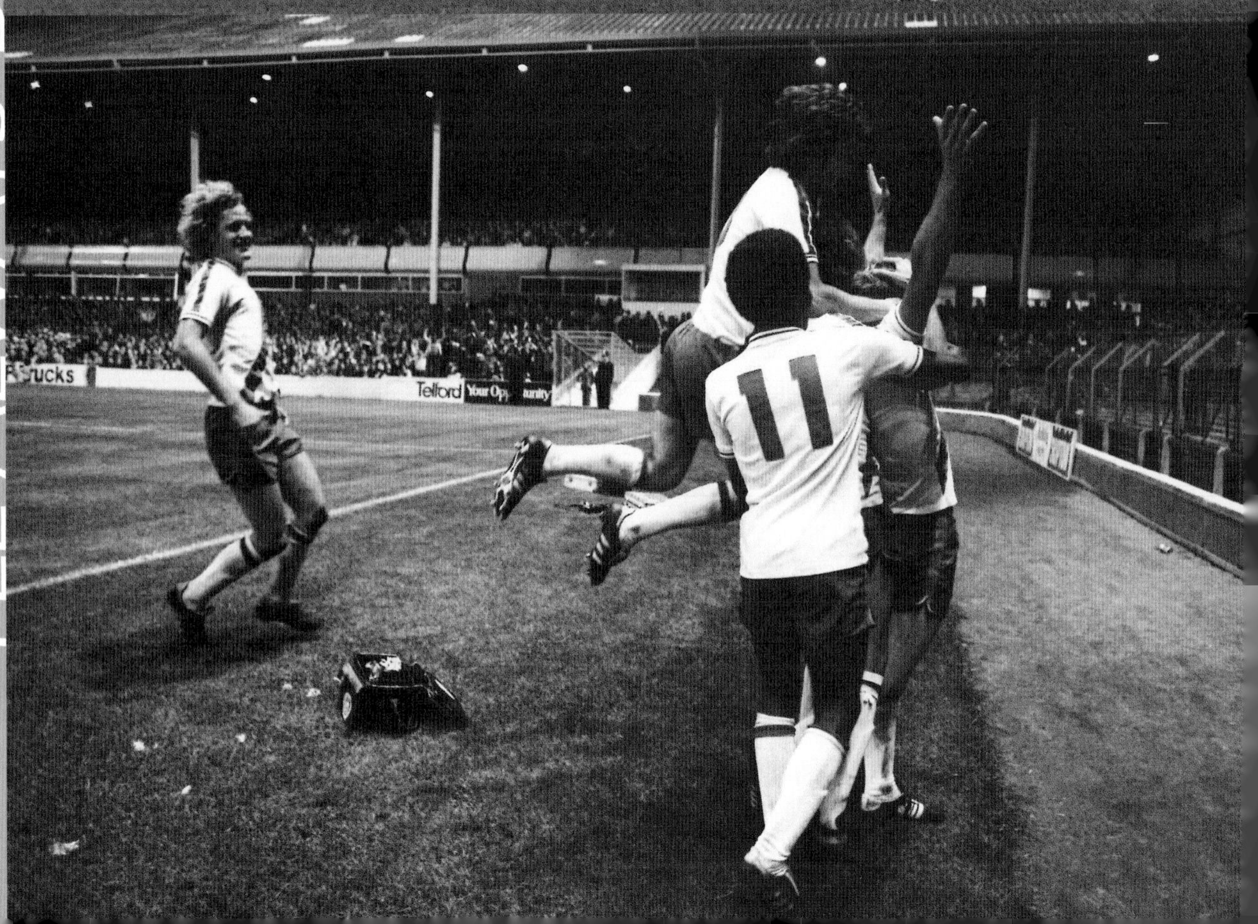

Gooooals.

Top Left: 33,685 witnessed this 'Swindles' special in the 3-1 win over Brighton in October '78.
Right: Vince catches Hy's 'eye'.

Bottom, Far Left: The game of two penalties. Nicky Chatterton celebrates with fans after converting his penalty at Villa Park in the League Cup, again in October '78. John Burridge saved their's and it went to a replay at Selhurst.

Below and Bottom Left: Mike Elwiss scores against West Ham at the start of a run that was to net him 5 goals in 6 games.

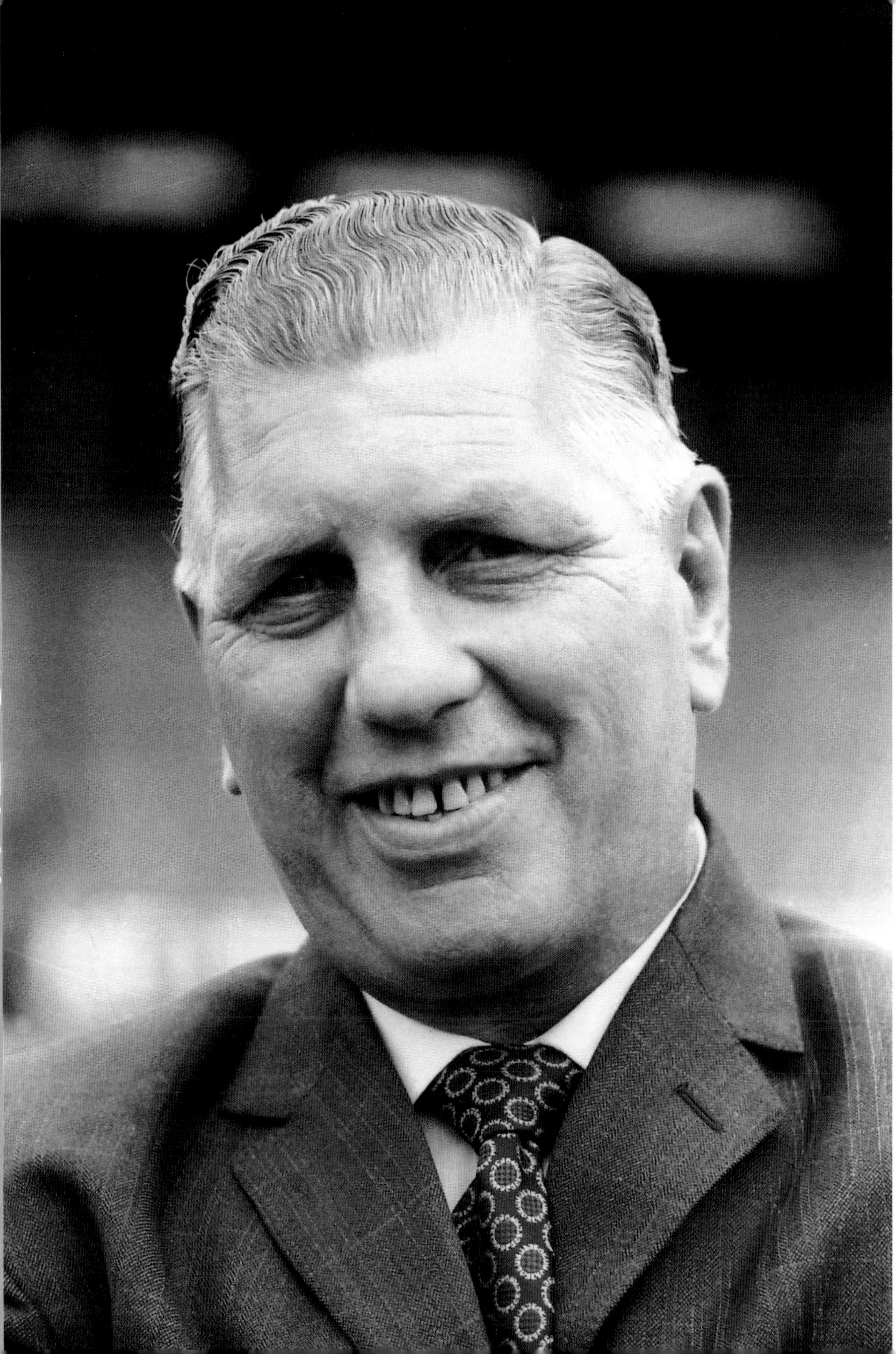

Bert Head reigned at the Palace from 14th April, 1966 to 30th March, 1973. As the first Manager to steer the club into the highest Division, he shall forever be remembered as a true Palace great. Many a fan will tell of his offers to travel home on the team coach and the consideration he gave to fans' letters. This relationship is brilliantly captured by Hy above.

CESSORIES FOR TAPE

Malcolm Allison was to a large degree the antithesis of what Crystal Palace had once been. Even the relative glamour we had become exposed to in the 60s and the 'Head'y ascent into the upper atmosphere was very different to the world Allison inhabited. His mantra in life – to have fun, be big and worry about consequences later – was imprinted on the Club in spades. His flamboyance kept the name of Crystal Palace in the Newspapers. His opinion that Palace should think of itself as a big club has become ingrained in the psyche of fans ever since. His other lasting legacy was the changing of our nick-name, which remains controversial. The Club, which was originally named after a building, had a fresh transfusion of energy as 'The Eagles'. Out went the White with Claret and Blue as well, replaced by the Red and Blue striped 'Barcelona' home shirt and an all White 'Real Madrid' Away kit. The fans have been dreaming of glory ever since.

THE GAFFER

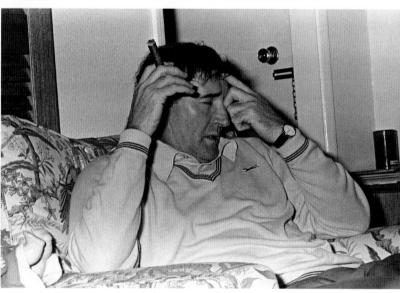

THE GAFFER

From that first shot of Malcolm on the day he arrived at Selhurst (see page 55), Hy clearly had a special affinity with him, much in evidence in some of these shots.

LEFT: Coach Terry with fans after the disappointment of missing out on promotion at Tranmere, 1975.

ABOVE: P.B. Yuill at his typewriter drafting out his latest 'cockney geezer' masterpiece *Hazell*, also adapted for the small screen.

FAR RIGHT: Sheepskin Manager, with Charlie

Simpson and Rach 'The Smash' Harkouk.

SEQUENCE BELOW: Above the players tunnel, in The Eagles Nest. Journalist Ken Jones keeps Tel company. Spot the lone expressionless spectator, completely unmoved while all around him lose their heads.

OVERLEAF: The many faces of 'El Tel'!

THE GAFFER

After Terry left on 30th October, 1980, Ernie Walley, a mainstay of the back room staff for years, took over as Caretaker Manager. In his 6 games in charge, Palace won the first (at home to Manchester United, 1-0) and forced a 2-2 draw against Liverpool at Selhurst. Unfortunately the other four were lost. The 80/81 season was spiralling out of control.

ABOVE: Although seen here with Clive Allen, the striker didn't play a single game during Ernie's brief tenure.

RIGHT: Ernie reviews press cuttings about possible Palace ventures into the transfer market.

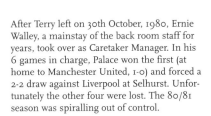

THE GAFFER

The return of 'Big Mal'.
ABOVE: Taking over from Ernie.
LEFT: Clive Allen, rejected by Walley, clearly welcomed Allison's arrival.

BELOW: Mal with his brother.
TOP LEFT AND RIGHT: Hy catches the strain with these intimate shots. The once friendly press had turned against him.

LEFT, RIGHT AND BELOW: And so arrived Dario Gradi, looking bemused by the rigours of the job he inherited from Malcolm.

PAGES 198-199 (TOP): After only 7 wins in 30 games, by November '81 Dario was superseded by Steve Kember. Steve's 12 wins in 37 included a gritty Cup run, ended, of all people, by Clive Allen who was back at QPR.

RIGHT AND BELOW: Alan Mullery, despised by most Palace fans for his Brighton connection, was unbelievably employed by Ron Noades to replace Steve Kember, who had not had the chance to get the Manager's chair warm. Mullery immediately faced his own 'Burnley' moment at the end of his first season, when Palace needed a draw to avoid the drop. Finishing 18th the following season wasn't good enough either.

PAGES 198-199 (BOTTOM): Enter Steve Coppell.

FOLLOWING PAGE: Now do these two gentle-men *love* each other, or what?

THE GAFFER

FAR LEFT: Steve Coppell at a Lifeline meeting.
FAR LEFT, BELOW: Steve with Ken Brown,
Manager of Norwich and formerly a player
with West Ham and England.

Other Palace Managers caught by Hy's lens:
LEFT TOP: Harry Bassett. Here for a day.
ABOVE: Ray Lewington.
ABOVE RIGHT: Alan Smith's loving cup.
BELOW: Trevor Francis.
RIGHT: The Dowie 'fist'.

PALACE COACHES, CLOCKWISE FROM TOP LEFT: Terry Long, Alan Harris (with Terry and Arnie Warren), John Cartwright, Martin Hinshelwood (right) and Alan Harris again.

THE GAFFER (COACHES)

THE GAFFER (COACHES)

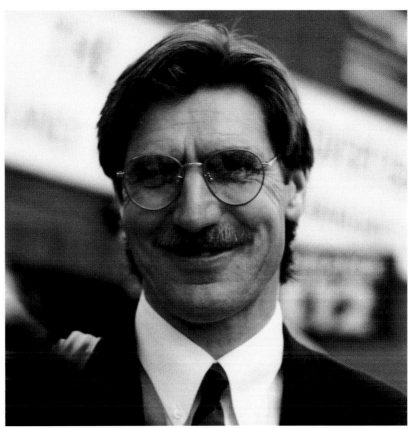

CLOCKWISE FROM LEFT: David Kemp with the First Division trophy; George Graham; Steve Harrison; Steve Coppell with 'Spike' Hill, Alan Smith and Ian Branfoot; Ian Evans (Paul Hinshelwood in foreground); Phil Holder.

LEFT: Mike Elwiss, a star in his sadly brief
Palace career.

ABOVE: All eyes are on Dave Swindlehurst,
including Hy's, who keeps him sharply in
focus.

LEFT: Nicky Chatterton, always hustling.

BELOW AND FAR RIGHT: Mike Elwiss overcoming hazardous loo paper as well as a close-marking opponent.

RIGHT: Jim Cannon.

Next 3 Pages: League Cup Replay against Villa in October, 1978 (0-0 after extra time).

TOP LEFT: Bicycle-kicking Vince Hilaire.

LEFT: Peter Nicholas.

ABOVE: Aerial ballet – Nicky Chatterton. Jerry Murphy looks on.

BELOW: Hinshelwood heads back accross goal toward Elwiss and 'Swindles'.

RIGHT: Terry Venables and Alan Harris ensure concentration is maintained for Extra Time. Dave Horn applies the 'magic sponge'.

OVERLEAF: Ian Walsh (top), Jerry Murphy (bottom left) and Billy Gilbert.

ABOVE: 1971-72 first team squad.

LEFT: The fresh-faced youth team prepare to embark on an U-21 tournament in Italy. Standing from left are Gary Towse, Jimbo, Martin and Paul Hinshelwood; in front, Len Prince on his suitcase and Keith Walley.

BELOW: It is fitting that Terry Long was influential in bringing through bright young stars such as Jim Cannon.

LEFT: A first team squad from early 1973 pose for Hy before setting off from Selhurst.

BELOW: The 71-72 youth team, pictured with some welcome additions to the silverware. Ernie Walley and Terry Long are the coaches.

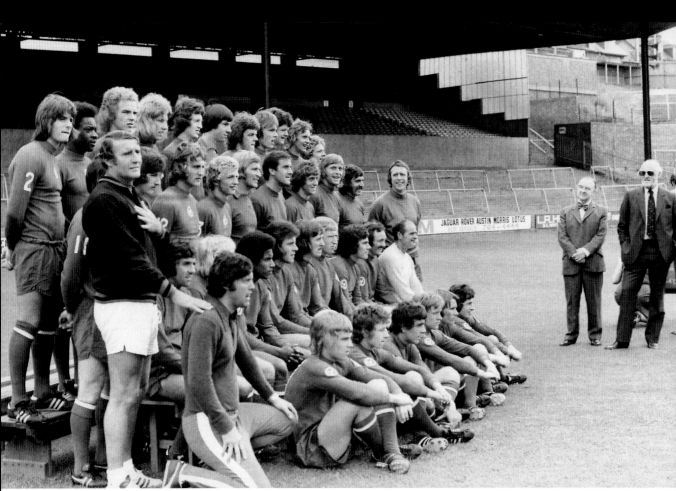

THIS SPREAD: Various shots from the 1974-75 photo-call.

ABOVE LEFT: Mark Lindsay.

ABOVE: Kenny Ayres, Stan Williams and Malcolm Beason. Kenny and Stan remained friends and both have spent time in Norway, where Stan still coaches today.

ABOVE: During 76-77 aspiring songstress Katy Budd paid a visit.

BELOW: Players (l-r) Ian Evans, Nicky Chatterton, Jeff Bourne, Tony Burns and Dave Swindlehurst line up alongside a lifelong Crystal Palace supporter.

ABOVE RIGHT: The team jet off for their tour of the States in the Summer of '79.

LEFT BELOW: Jeff Bourne, Phil Holder, Ian Evans and Nicky Chatterton.

ABOVE: After the 2nd Division Championship had been secured, the team gathers in the Social Club.

BELOW: Before the 5-0 demolition of Chelsea in a pre-season friendly, 1979.

Peter Caswell

Tony Burns

Ian Evans

Billy Gilbert

Kenny Sansom

Paul Hinshelwood

Nick Chatterton

George Graham

Phil Holder

Peter Nicholas

Neil Smillie

Vince Hilaire

Rachid Harkouk

Ian Walsh

Steve Perrin

Dave Swindlehurst

Jeff Bourne

LEFT: Portraits of the promotion squad taken during pre-season 77-78, including Peter 'The Mad Monk' Caswell!

RIGHT: Snazzy numbers in the wall versus QPR – where's the keeper?

RIGHT MIDDLE: Vince Hilaire, Jim Cannon, Jerry Murphy, Henry Hughton and Shaun Brooks reverting to red and blue stripes for 83-84.

BELOW: Weeping willows – a rural setting for the 80/81 team group.

Apart from Steve Kember in action against Portsmouth (right), Hy took all these at Upton Park in November '78.

TOP LEFT: Ian Walsh and Mike Elwiss (Elwiss came on as substitute and was Palace's scorer in a 1-1 draw).

LEFT: Dave Swindlehurst.

ABOVE: A West Ham attack breaks down. Steve Kember issues instructions as Trevor Brooking turns away. The referee is Mr Kirkpatrick of Leicester, whose exaggerated antics, particularly running backwards at great speed, were always amusing but distracting (what exactly is he doing *here*, one wonders?).

TOP RIGHT: Billy Bonds tries to block Jim Cannon's shot, watched by the bearded Frank Lampard (Senior!).

Nearly 20,000 pack into Brisbane Road as Palace take on Orient in the last away game of Championship-winning season 78-79.

TOP LEFT: Ralph Coates was one of few non-ex-Palace players taking part. Here, he lets Jim Cannon know he's about.

FAR LEFT: Coates is superbly caught in hair flying action. At that time, he and Bobby Charlton vied for the best 'comb-over'.

NEAR LEFT: The legendary John Jackson. Painful for older Palace fans to see him in enthusiastic action for Orient.

ABOVE: Sansom, Nicholas (no.7) and Fenwick watch as Billy Gilbert climbs over an Orient striker to clear.

RIGHT: Vince Hilaire with Henry Hughton.

ABOVE: 'Swindles' on ice at the Goldstone, Brighton, Boxing Day '79.

RIGHT: A pre-planned free-kick routine. Tony Hazell positions the ball for the signalling Steve Kember to take.

BELOW: A permed Dave Swindlehurst is caught in a Lions sandwich by Barry Kitchener and keeper Nicky Johns. Johns now works in the 'Palace In The Community' team.

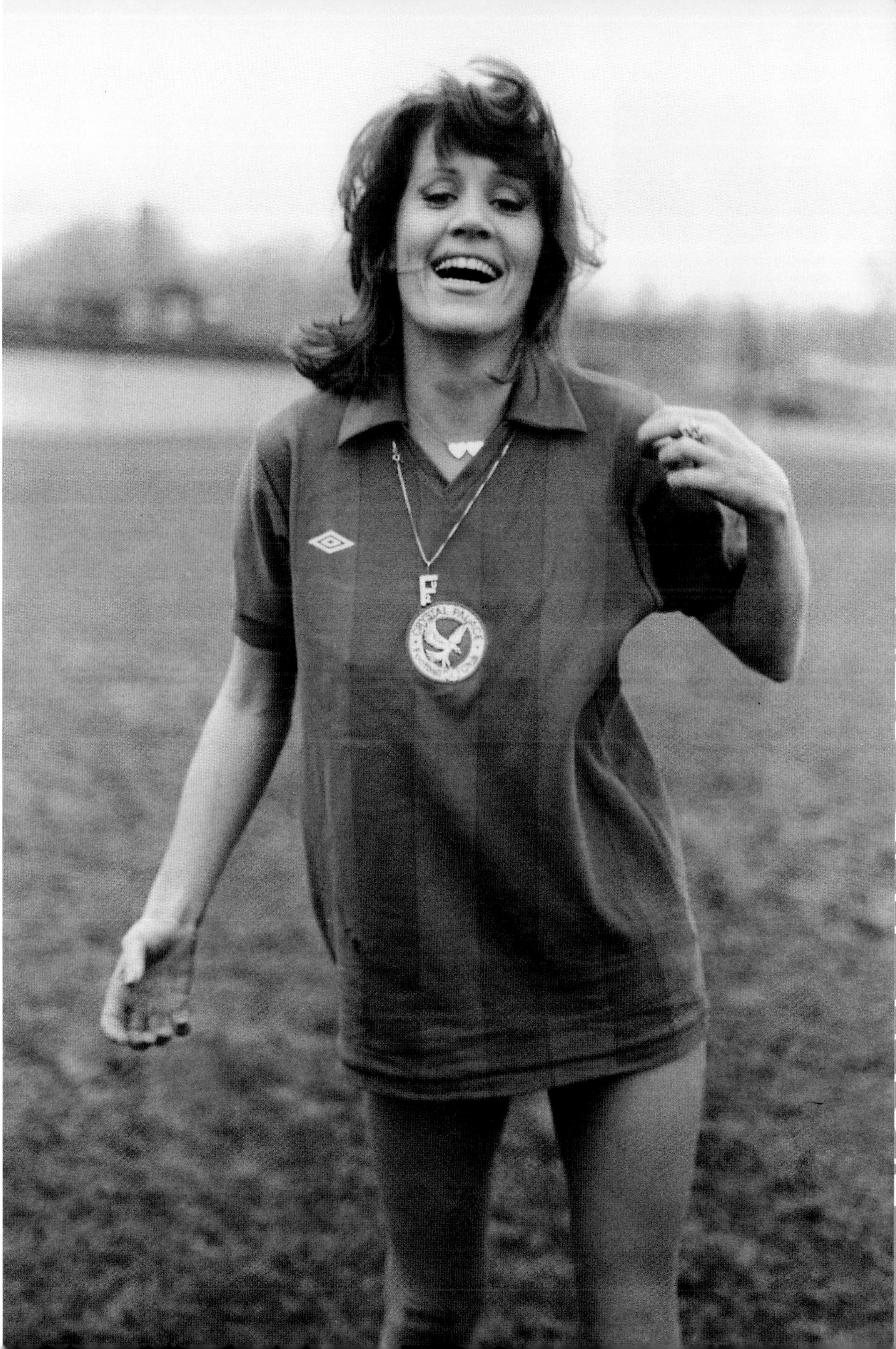

# FIONA AND OTHER NICE LADIES

Glamour model Fiona Richmond
arrives at the training ground in
Paul Raymond's Rolls Royce, wearing no more than her Palace shirt,
kinky boots and knickers.

FIONA AND OTHER NICE LADIES

LEFT: Fiona shows Malcolm the way forward.

THIS PAGE: Palace Ladies football team.

ABOVE: An impressive collection of trophies won by the Palace Ladies during their first two years!

BELOW: The Palace lasses doing a 'Fiona'.

TOP RIGHT: Synchronised training methods.

MIDDLE RIGHT: Early, claret and blue action.

BOTTOM RIGHT: Captain Sue Head.

FIONA AND OTHER NICE LADIES

The Palace Dollies.

ABOVE: Shirley Saville, the main Palace Dollies co-ordinator is standing on the left with Chair Jackie Foster in front of her and Secretary Mary Carter standing on the right. The Ladies section at the Club was an extension of the buzzing social scene and helped set up the original Christmas party in '69, originally intended for pensioners.

RIGHT: Two all-time Palace greats together on 29th March, 1980 as Palace confront Manchester United at Selhurst.

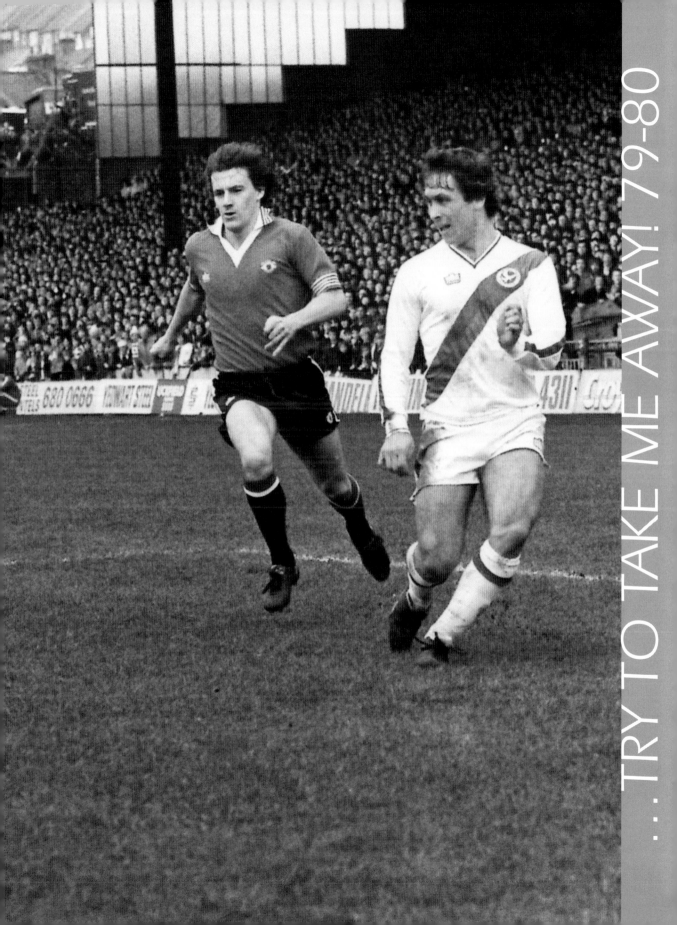

THERE AND BACK AGAIN! After 6 years and 4 months, top flight football returned to Selhurst with the visit of Southampton.

RIGHT: 'King' Kenny Sansom.

FACING PAGE, TOP LEFT: Vince 'The Prince' Hilaire, seen here leaping over Paul Cooper of Ipswich.

TOP RIGHT: In the same, historic game, Jim Cannon in action, with England's Terry Butcher in the background.

FACING PAGE, BOTTOM: 'The Prince' fires in a shot on goal.

TOP LEFT: Vince Hilaire and Argentinian Ricky Villa of Spurs.

LEFT: Mike Flanagan gets in a cross under pressure from Don McAllister of Spurs.

ABOVE: Mike Flanagan dives to flick a header past the outstretched boot of Scotland captain Martin Buchan.

LEFT: Ian Walsh at Old Trafford with Sammy McIlroy, Kevin Moran and Ray Wilkins.

RIGHT: Ian again at Old Trafford, rushing to meet a right-wing cross ahead of Kevin Moran.

BOTTOM LEFT: This time Ian evades Gordon McQueen to fire a shot on goal in the return game at Selhurst.

BOTTOM RIGHT: Ian yet again puts United under pressure.

BELOW: This time it's Mike Flanagan firing in a shot on the United goal, watched by Vince Hilaire and Peter Nicholas.

TOP LEFT: Vince fends off Wolves' Derek Parkin.
LEFT: 'Jimbo'.
ABOVE: Brighton's Brian Horton flinches from Paul Hinshelwood's bicycle-kick.
BELOW: Vince sees off Gerry Ryan, Peter

O'Sullivan and Horton.
TOP RIGHT: Jim Cannon in an aerial duel with
Steve Foster.
RIGHT: Gerry Francis glides past a Coventry
opponent and into the penalty area.

HUNKS

LEFT: Kenny Sansom.
BELOW, MAIN PICTURE: Don Rogers
LEFT, TOP: Peter Nicholas.
LEFT, BOTTOM: Derek Possee.

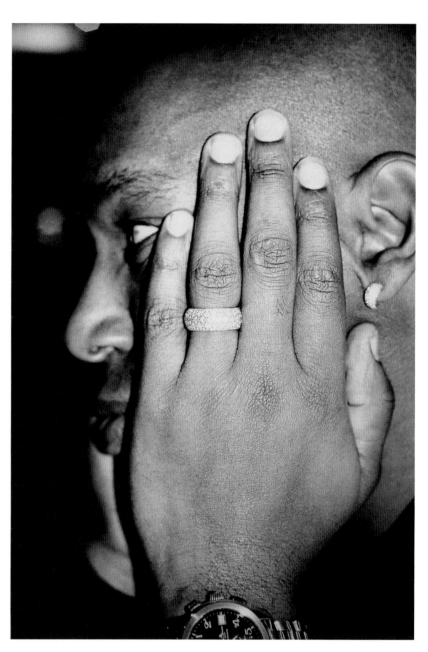

WRIGHT and...

ABOVE LEFT: Fabrizio Bilio.

LEFT: Alan Pardew.

...BRIGHT

ABOVE RIGHT: Shaun Brooks

RIGHT: Alan Birchenall.

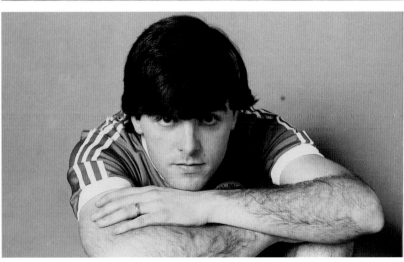

HUNKS

Hunks

This Spread, Clockwise from Top Left:
Dean Gordon; Chris Armstrong; Chris
Coleman; Eric Young; Geoff Thomas; Gareth
Southgate.

Overleaf, Clockwise from Left:
Clive Allen; Gerry Francis; Paul Hinshelwood;
Bobby Kellard.

ABOVE: Peter Taylor.
TOP RIGHT: Jim Scott.
RIGHT: Barry Silkman.
OPPOSITE: Kenny Sansom.

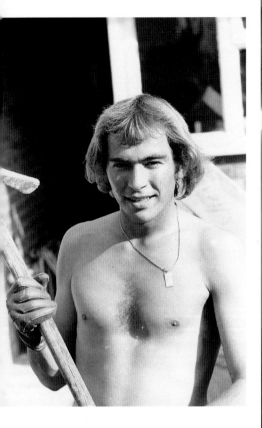

CLOCKWISE FROM ABOVE: Gavin Nebbeling; Mel Blyth; Ian Wright; Steve Coppell.

OPPOSITE: Ian Wright perfectly evades Bruce Grobbelaar.

TOP LEFT: 'The DreamTeam'. Mark Bright, Steve Coppell and Ian Wright.

ABOVE: Wright & Bright – still crazy after all these years.

LEFT: Ian and Mark's proud mums.

BELOW AND OPPOSITE: ... with Alex Dyer (centre).

THIS SPREAD: The family Noades.

ABOVE LEFT AND ABOVE RIGHT: Joining 'The Last Stand', the Noades' blend in with the Holmesdale enders.

LEFT: With a growing trophy collection.

RIGHT AND BELOW: Ron Noades willingly pays the price for losing his bet against 'Brightie' scoring a hat-trick.

ABOVE: Novello backs her husband.

OVERLEAF: Watford were the visitors in May, 1994 for the final game before the double-decker stand was erected at the Holmesdale Road end. 'Colour-full' for the last time.

HY IN COLOUR 2

THIS SPREAD: 8th May, 1994. Palace are Champs and the Holmesdale Road terrace, after 70 years of service, is to be dismantled.

ABOVE: Chris Armstrong scored an impressive 22 goals during the season.

BOTTOM FAR LEFT: Nigel 'Stretch' Martyn with his medal.

BOTTOM NEAR LEFT: Bruce Dyer with the trophy.

BELOW: The 'White Horse' and the Holmesdale.

LEFT: Hy always cut a dash in her red, white and blue jacket.

BELOW: 30 years exactly after being relegated to the old 3rd Division at Ninian Park, Palace are back in Cardiff, winning the Play-Off Final at The Millenium Stadium and returning to the Premier Division.

ABOVE AND RIGHT: In the penultimate home game of 2004-05, Andy Johnson offered a crucial lifeline with this incredible glancing header against Liverpool. 'AJ' shows appreciation for play-maker Wayne Routledge.

THIS SPREAD: The Premier Division 2004-05.

ABOVE: Hy's timing is perfect as Gabor Kiraly just fails to reach Peter Crouch's penalty.

RIGHT: Aki Riihilahti and Milan Baros.

SEQUENCE, LEFT TO RIGHT, BOTTOM:
Tom Soares; Wayne Routledge; Nicola Ventola; Michael Hughes; Danny Butterfield; Mikele Leigertwood; Michael Hughes.

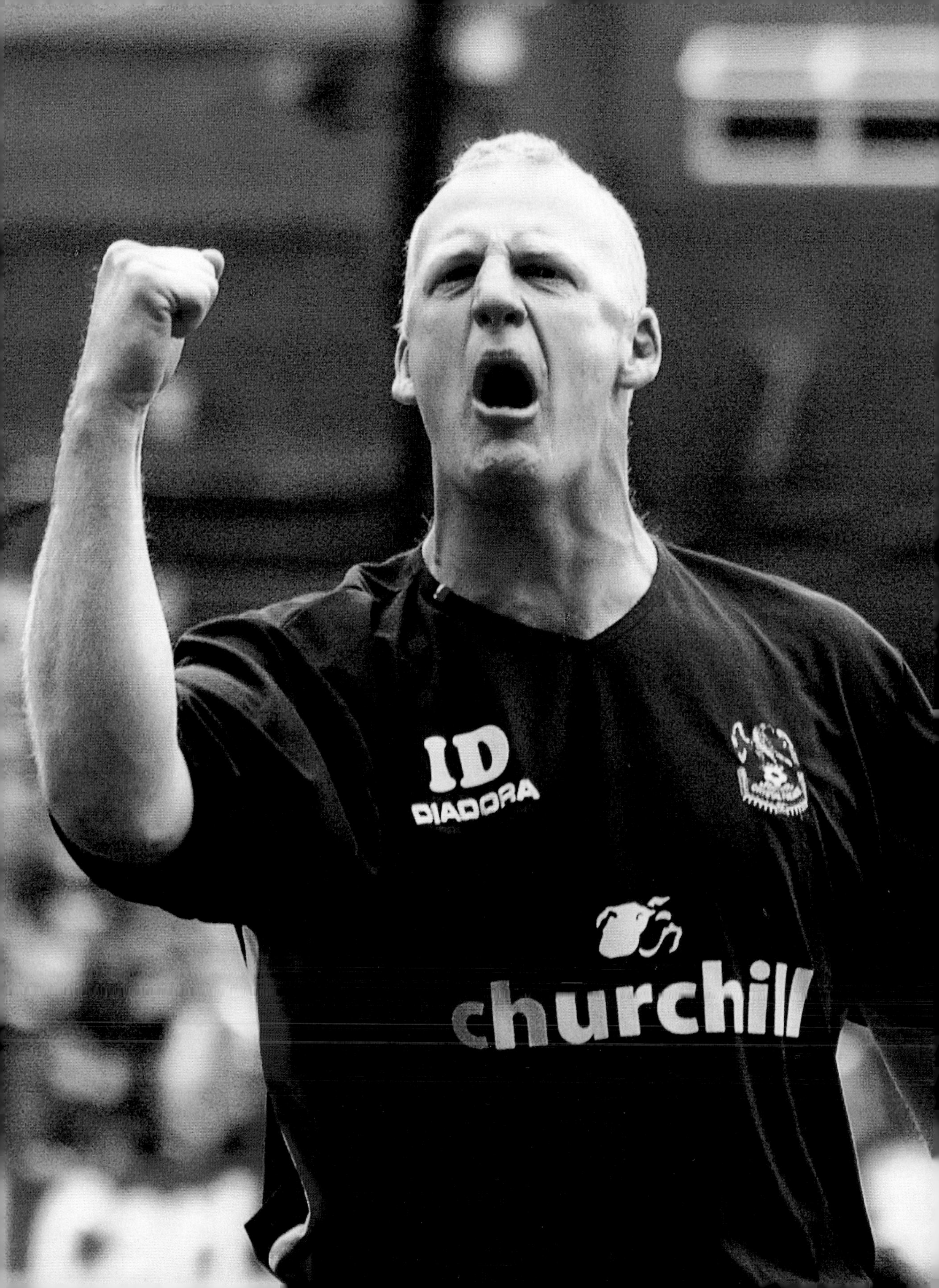
ID
DIADORA
churchill

LEFT: After Iain Dowie made a spontaneous 'salute' with his fist, following a win at Portman Road, it became expected whenever Palace won thereafter. This one after a 1-0 defeat of Liverpool meant more than most.

ABOVE, CLOCKWISE FROM TOP LEFT: Danny Granville; Gabor Kiraly; Ben Watson; Tony Popovic; Tom Soares; Aki Riihilahti; Fitz Hall; Mikele Leigertwood.

BELOW LEFT: Geoff Thomas – all time Palace hero, pictured at Selhurst in 2005.

BELOW: Bob, Iain and proud mother Ann Dowie.

THIS PAGE: Iain Dowie consoles a distrought Andy Johnson after Premiership survival appeared to have been wrestled from Palace's clutches with a cruel last minute Southampton goal.

OPPOSITE: The team celebrate Ian Walsh's goal against Tottenham in front of a bumper 45,296 crowd at Selhurst.

IT'S BY YOUR SIDE I WILL STAY 79-81

ABOVE: Having just scored one of the most perfect goals ever witnessed at Selhurst, Jim Cannon does a 'Charlie George'.

LEFT: 'Jimbo' climbs to his feet and celebrates triumphantly with Kenny Sansom. His volley followed sweet interplay as Palace beat Ipswich 4-1. Palace hit the crest of the wave and go top for one short week before crashing back down to earth.

LEFT: This sublime, golden moment was captured by Hy. TV appears oblivious to the momentous TV moment.

BELOW: More joy at Selhurst as the team celebrate a cool Gerry Francis penalty conversion.

THIS PAGE: 1980-81 was to bring sorrow and suffering back to the faithful, although, as with this celebration of a Mike Flanagan goal, it did have some *Hys*!

OPPOSITE: Len Chatterton's wife Betty and her sister Madge at work, washing the kit.

WE WORK HERE TOO

RIGHT: The St. John's Ambulance men and women are unsung heroes at football grounds and major events all over the country. This gentleman was a long-serving senior member of No.221 Addiscombe (St John's) Ambulance Division.

BELOW: Keeping the Glaziers crest shining (inside the main entrance).

TOP RIGHT: Charlie Simpson, our hard working physio, 'invades' the pitch at White Hart Lane.

BOTTOM RIGHT: Vic Worrall, Selhurst Park Stadium Manager shares a break with Beryl Whitfield, latterly with the Club Shop. Between them they have given over half a century of service to the Club.

WE WORK HERE TOO

LEFT: It's a tough job. Malcolm Holmes and Les Barnes – Stewards with a smile!

BELOW: Barry Williams, whose immense contribution to the cause at Gentlemens' Evenings and Lifeline 'do's epitomises the humour all Palace fans need to survive.

LEFT: Bill Harrison, with his cheery smile and easy, laconic, Irish charm has often lightened the gloom after another dismal defeat.

ABOVE AND BELOW: Let's hear it for Len! Mr. Chatterton has been a mainstay at the Palace longer than anyone can remember, including Len himself! He is still active taking children's parties on matchdays and is fondly renowned as 'Leo The Clown' at the Xmas parties. It is unlikely anyone has put in as many man-hours for the Palace cause, with over 60 years service to the Club. He is the father of former player Nick.

WE WORK HERE TOO

ABOVE:
THE TEAM BEHIND MAL'S TEAM.
BELOW:
THE TEAM BEHIND TERRY'S TEAM.

OVERLEAF, ABOVE LEFT: Overcoming the flu are Peter Barnes, Renee Collins, Chris Hassell, (unidentified) and Bert Wait.
BOTTOM LEFT: Club Secretary Alan Leather and the Palace doctors celebrate promotion.
MIDDLE, ABOVE: Mike 'Hurstie' Hurst, still alive in the ticket office.

BELOW: Ken the Commissionaire with Peter Broughton and Ted Gammons.
ABOVE RIGHT: Some of The Supporters Club Committee. Back Row: Reg Watts, Mick Ryan, Brian Simpson (Shop), Gerry O'Shea, Ken

Wilson. Seated: Fred Pratt (President), Mickey Pratt (Travel), Stan Whitby (Hon. Secretary). BOTTOM RIGHT: Alan Leather tinkling the ivories with an impressed Tony Shaw.

LEFT: Beryl, Lyn and Chris, all part of the Palace family.

BELOW LEFT: Alan Leather (AJL).

BELOW: John Matthews (left of this group) gave many years service to Palace fans with his excellent and comprehensive Palace reporting in the Croydon Advertiser.

WE WORK HERE TOO

WHO LET THE DUG OUT?

THE AGONY AND THE ECSTASY.
LEFT: Charlie Simpson, TV, John Cartwright, Alan Whittle and Dave Horn.
ABOVE: Peter Wall with TV.
BELOW: Tony Sealy, Alan Harris, TV and Dave Horn.

WHO LET THE DUG OUT?

RIGHT: Neil Smillie, TV, Alan Harris and (background) Charlie Simpson.
BOTTOM RIGHT: Horn, TV and Harris again.

WHO LET THE DUG OUT?

LEFT: Malcolm Allison with Dave Horn.

BOTTOM LEFT: Allison in discussion with Charlie Simpson.

LEFT: Going for a 'Burton'. The new look tunnel lacked the class of the original.

BELOW: Len Chatterton, (unidentified), Ian Evans, Ernie Walley and Charlie Simpson.

ABOVE: Put your gum away, Alan! Jerry Murphy is on the left and Coach Ken Shellito sits forward to the right.

BELOW: Dave Horn, Ricky Heppolette, Martin Hinshelwood and Peter Wall.

TOP RIGHT: Martin, Anthony and Stuart Money prepare for their 'trial'!

BOTTOM RIGHT: After Blackburn 89 – 'Was That It?'

SEQUENCE FAR RIGHT:
Stevie Coppell and 'Taff' Evans – a tough first year in management for both of them.

ABOVE: A young Ian Wright waiting for his big chance.

BOTTOM LEFT: Maurice Drewitt, Micky Droy, Steve and Ian.

BOTTOM RIGHT: Nigel Martyn, Richard Shaw,

John Pemberton, Geoff Thomas and Ian Wright again.

OPPOSITE: Mike Flanagan, Jim Cannon and Paul Hinshelwood.

WHO LET THE DUG OUT?

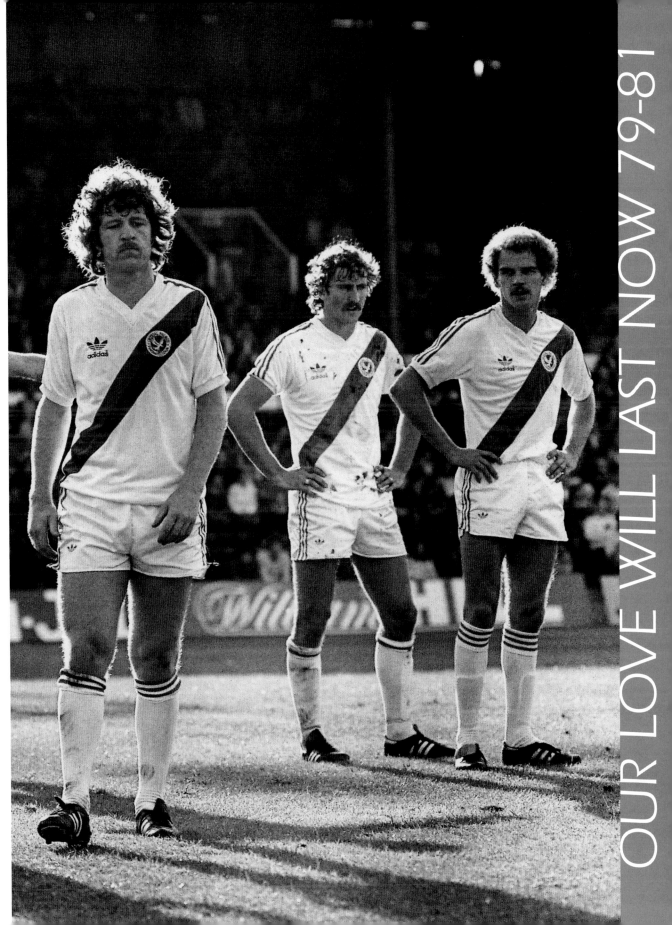

OUR LOVE WILL LAST NOW 79-81

ABOVE LEFT AND LEFT: In his own right, Clive Allen was a good enough replacement for the much-missed Swindlehurst, but the loss of Sansom was a bitter blow. The pairing of Flanagan and Allen was manna for the media but the duo failed to 'hit the boards' running. In 13 starts together, other than a hat-trick apiece, they only managed three other goals between them – all from Allen (and one of them, at Coventry, was not even awarded by the referee!). On the left Clive tries to pounce but Ipswich 'keeper Paul Cooper and George Burley have it covered.

ABOVE: Vince Hilaire, Clive Allen and Gerry Francis plan a free kick.

TOP RIGHT: Allen attempts a spectacular shot.

RIGHT: Preparations for extra time against Spurs in the League Cup.

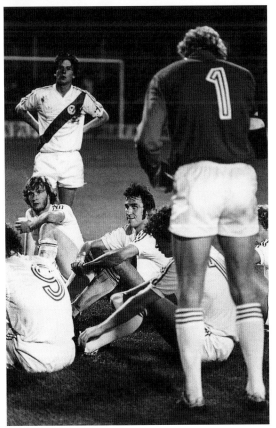

ABOVE: The trademark Kenny Sansom long throw.

LEFT: 'Doris' gets personal with Phil Boyer of Southampton.

RIGHT: Hy's famous crowd scene, taken in the early '70s is still hugely evocative of the era.

WE ALL FOLLOW THE PALACE

THIS PAGE, 'CREATURE' COMFORTS:

BELOW: Now who would bring a lovely dog like that to a place like this? Chris Wright of course!

OPPOSITE, TOP RIGHT: Coppers and cameras always get the best view 'in the house'.

BOTTOM RIGHT: The Whitehorse wall end after the paint job.

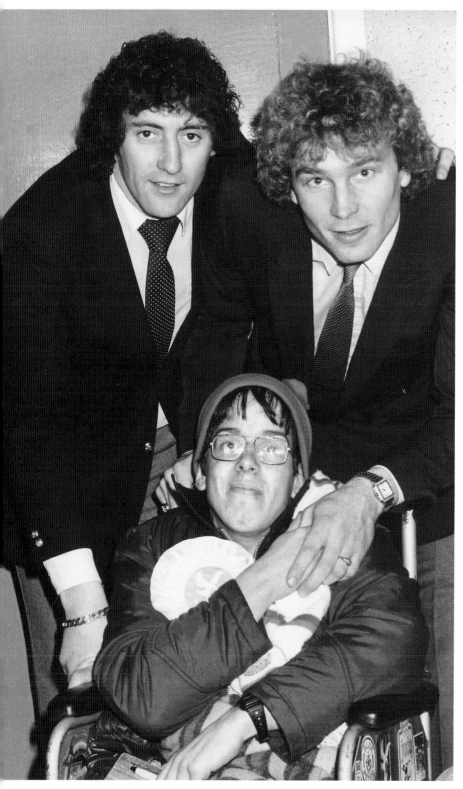

LEFT: Palace fanatic Richard, with the permed pairing of Terry Boyle and Paul Barron.

ABOVE: Vince meets his fans, including a young David Halfacre behind him.

BELOW LEFT: Ian Edwards gets a pat on the head as he leaves the field.

ABOVE: David Payne signs for the fans.

BELOW: It's David again, this time at a player reunion, pointing out his grandfather in Hy's crowd scene photo (see p.297). On the right is Bobby Kellard.

WE ALL FOLLOW THE PALACE

RIGHT AND BELOW: The Holmesdale – those boards took one hell of a beating once "Glad All Over" came out over the tannoy.

OPPOSITE: Joy and Payne, are like sunshine and rain.

LEFT: What d'you mean, am I Scottish?

BELOW: A young hoodlum gets away with John Jackson's wallet.

ABOVE: The away fans 'take' the Whitehorse tea bar.

 308

RIGHT: Having left Palace to join opponents QPR, John Burridge's minder helps him out during the explosive Cup Quarter Final at Loftus Road.

BELOW: LeSaux gets lairy, the crowd get hairy and Crouch... is off!

ABOVE LEFT: Ball boys come out of their hut – and into action!

LEFT: Lazy days.

ABOVE: Remember the days of scarves round the wrist?

WE ALL FOLLOW THE PALACE

BELOW: They grow so tall these days.

ABOVE RIGHT: Go on, I dare you – to the other side in 15 seconds.

BOTTOM RIGHT: We are all prisoners here – usually of our dad's device.

ABOVE LEFT: Moonstompin'.

BOTTOM LEFT: 'Ello, 'ello – it's Jethro.

ABOVE: Bridging the generations.

TOP RIGHT: I used to be a Wolves fan – but

I'm all right "nooooow".

BELOW: Jethro brings Cleggy (who is in fact supporter Keith Payne's dad).

BOTTOM RIGHT: The riot police on their day off.

# 'TIL THE END OF TIME 81-86

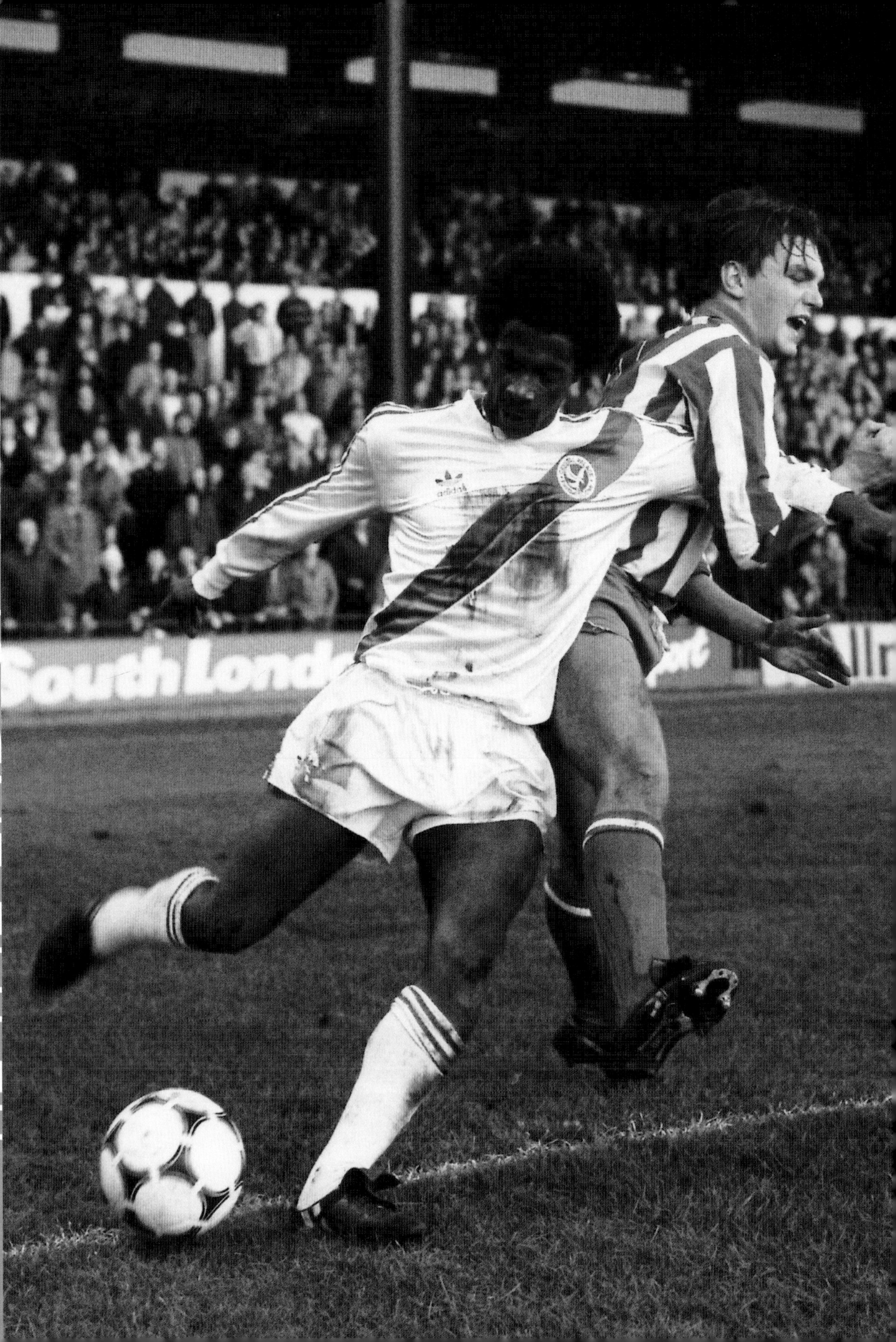

OPPOSITE: Hair AND Flair (Vince gets in a cross despite the armlock).

ABOVE : Kevin Mabbutt and Shaun Brooks.

ABOVE RIGHT: Neil Smillie sees off Terry Fenwick of QPR.

BELOW: Ian Walsh is robbed at the last gasp.

RIGHT: Brian Flynn of Burnley attempts a rugby tackle on Vince Hilaire.

LEFT: Orient's Henry Hughton props up the bar while Steve Wicks conducts the regulars.

BELOW: Ian Edwards bending over backwards in a Cup Tie against Burnley. Chris Jones is in the centre.

ABOVE AND ABOVE RIGHT: Jim Cannon has a quiet 'word' with the official. Other Palace players involved (l-r in the two shots) are Shaun Brooks, Ian Walsh, Neil Smillie and Jerry Murphy.

BELOW: Kevin Mabbutt gets ready to burst into action, marked closely by Orient's Tommy Taylor.

RIGHT: Getting into a tangle here are David Price and Tommy Langley.

OPPOSITE, TOP: Kevin Mabbutt fires past the lunge of Oldham Athletic's Paul Futcher.

OPPOSITE, BOTTOM: Tommy Langley crosses from the byeline against Sheffield Wednesday.

LEFT: Henry Hughton, who had left Orient to join Palace, gets involved in a clash of perms with Newcastle's Kevin Keegan.

BOTTOM LEFT: David Giles, the flying Welshman, with a fine effort against Derby County.

RIGHT: Brian Sparrow with Asa Hartford.

BELOW: Playing against Luton Town, Neil Smillie appears to grow an extra hand.

ABOVE: No.9 just bounces off him as Micky Droy, the colossus, heads clear.

RIGHT: Andy Gray gets Airborne.

BELOW: Ian Wright with his future Arsenal teammate Lee Dixon, then of Stoke City, in close attendance.

OPPOSITE: Tony 'Finn' Finnigan in full-flight.

IN THE FAMILY WAY

Opposite and Above: In safe hands... John Jackson with his daughter and, above, at Steve Kember's wedding – careful 'Jacko'. Apart from 'Jacko', left to right above are: Steve Kember himself, Phil Hoadley, David Payne, Mel Blyth and Alan Birchenall.

Left: 'Confetti Ken' and Elaine.

Below: Arthur Wait giving the bride away, with Bert Head in attendance.

IN THE FAMILY WAY

Doting mums and dads.

OPPOSITE TOP: Gerry Queen

OPPOSITE, FAR LEFT: Mike Hurst.

OPPOSITE, NEAR LEFT: Steve Kember.

ABOVE: Kenny Sansom.

LEFT: Alan Pinkney.

BELOW: Peter Nicholas.

IN THE FAMILY WAY

Happy Families.

<small>ABOVE:</small> John 'Yogi' Hughes.

<small>ABOVE RIGHT:</small> Mark Lindsay.

<small>RIGHT:</small> Tony Taylor.

<small>BOTTOM RIGHT:</small> Bobby Kellard.

<small>BELOW:</small> Terry Long.

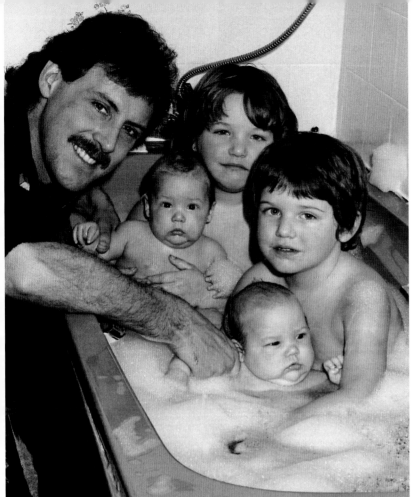

LEFT: David Swindlehurst.
ABOVE: Paul Hinshelwood.
BELOW: Steve Kember.

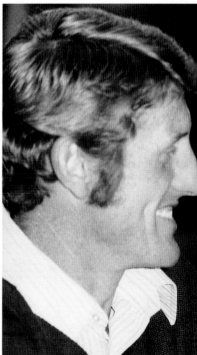

 330

With their wives.

OPPOSITE: John Jackson.

OPPOSITE, BOTTOM LEFT: Andy Thorn.

OPPOSITE, BOTTOM RIGHT: Geoff Thomas.

ABOVE: Clive Allen.

LEFT: Chris Coleman.

BELOW: John McCormick.

RIGHT: Alan Whittle.

BOTTOM, NEAR RIGHT: Malcolm Allison.

BOTTOM, FAR RIGHT: Ian Wright.

ABOVE LEFT: Ian Evans.

ABOVE: Alan Whittle.

LEFT: Martin Hinshelwood.

BELOW: Ray Bloye.

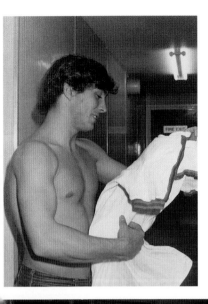

ABOVE LEFT: Kenny Sansom. Just a minute, that's no baby, that's an England shirt!

ABOVE: Ron Noades.

LEFT: John McCormick.

BELOW: John Burridge.

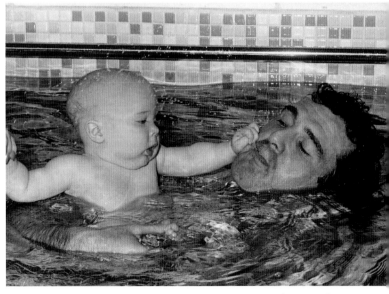

ABOVE: Terry Venables and dad Fred.

RIGHT: Three generations of Coppells here –
Steve with son Mark and dad, Frank.

 334

ABOVE: Ross Jenkins.

ABOVE MIDDLE: Ian Walsh.

ABOVE RIGHT: Jim Cannon.

BELOW: Eddie McGoldrick.

RIGHT: Don Rogers.

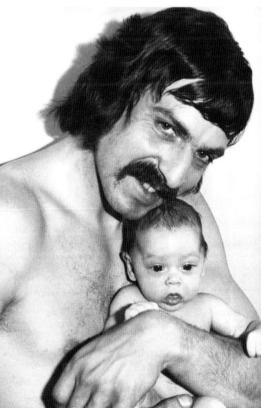

IN THE FAMILY WAY

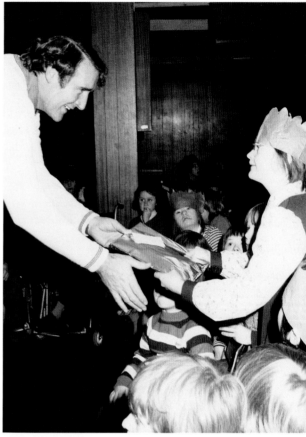

THIS PAGE: Malcolm Allison and Len 'Leo the Clown' Chatterton help make the Children's Christmas Party a memorable one.

OPPOSITE:
Giving up their time for Radio Mayday are (clockwise, from top left): John and Cathy Jackson; Martin, Wally and Paul Hinshelwood with Lindy, Jean and Rita Hinshelwood; Serena Williams and Mal; Mel 'n' Hy: Tony Taylor.

Chris Winter and Roger Dickson still broadcast their own inimitable matchday commentaries for Radio Mayday listeners.

337

# BECAUSE THIS LOVE IS 83-85

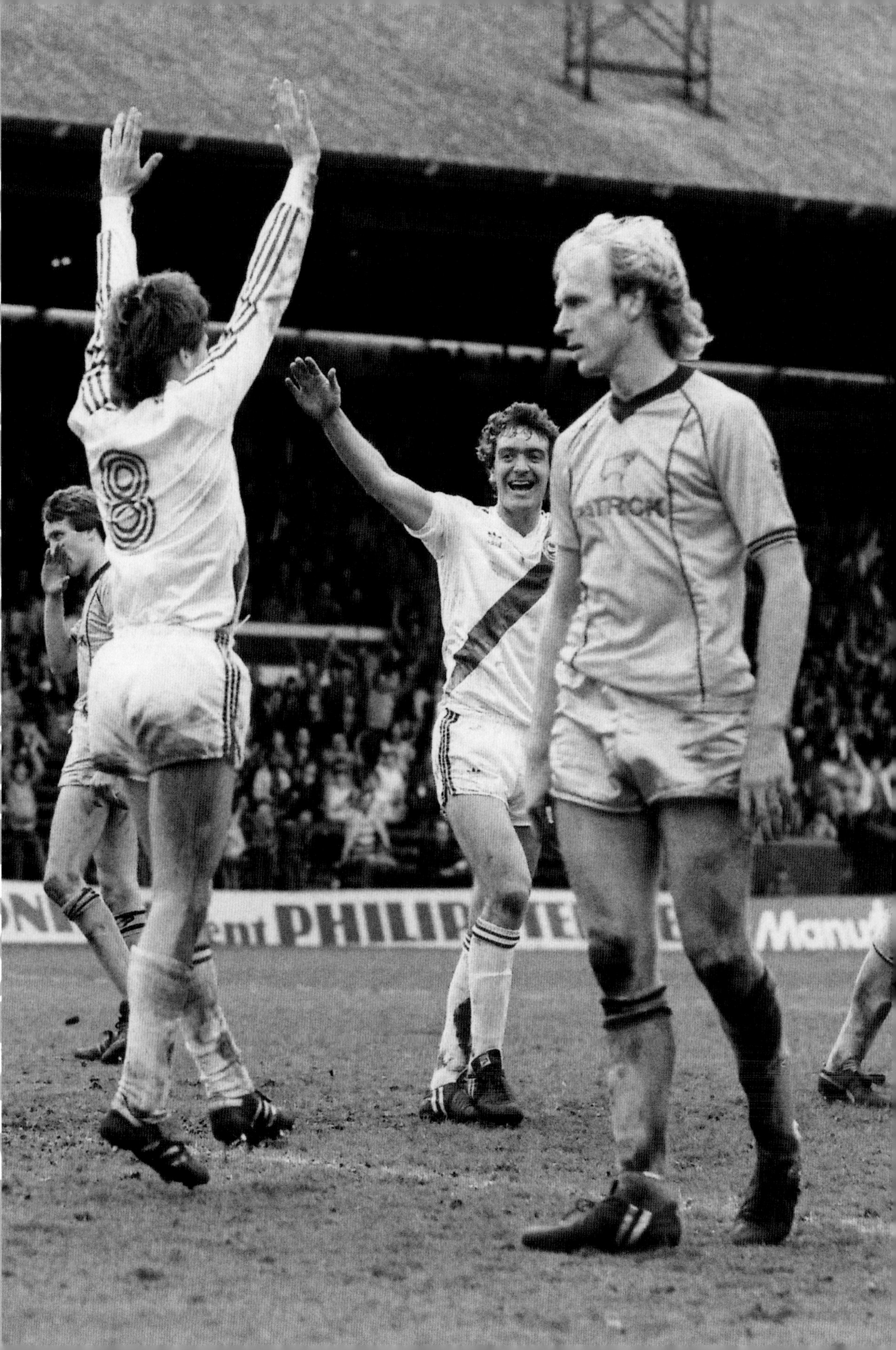

LEFT: Kevin Mabbutt celebrates one of his two vital goals against Derby with Alistair Brown.

ABOVE AND BELOW: In the same game, Henry Hughton makes it 4-1, giving Palace a vital lifeline for survival.

RIGHT: Andy McCulloch scores against Newcastle in a 3-1 victory for Palace. Peter Nicholas gets to his feet.

ABOVE: Delight at the Holmesdale end.

BELOW: Tony Finnigan celebrates a sweet victory against old rivals Millwall in September, 1985. A dejected Steve Lovell (once of the Palace) is on the right.

OPPOSITE: Flanked by Ian Walsh and Kenny Sansom, Terry Venables triumphantly acknowledges the super-sized, Selhurst sell-out crowd of 51,801 after clinching the Championship in May '79.

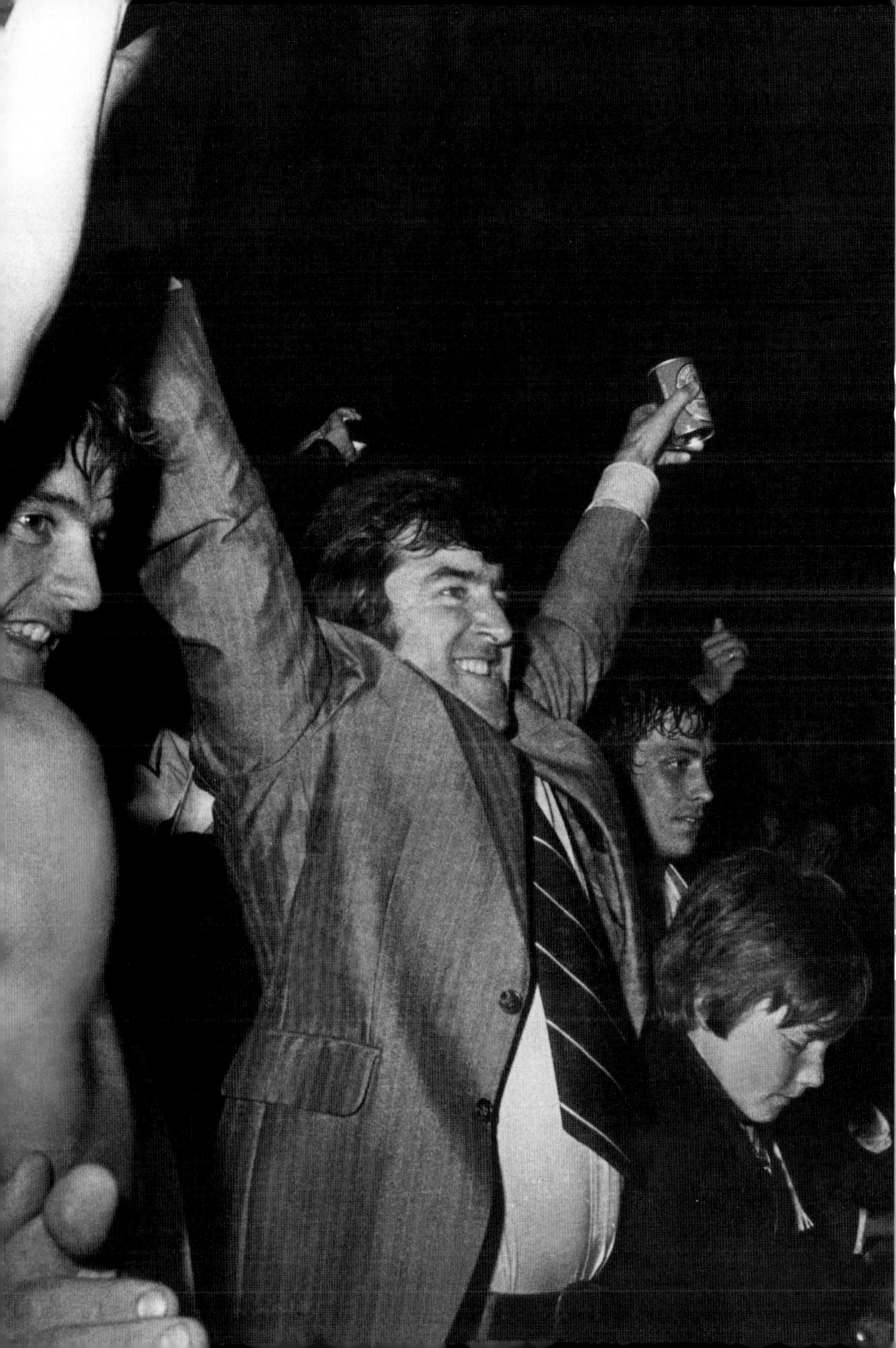

THIS SPREAD, PALACE V. BURNLEY, MAY '79: Finally! The Ian Walsh breakthrough goal, a thrilling, diving header on 76 minutes, sees him engulfed by jubilant team mates. OVERLEAF: The crowd ecstatically invade the pitch and Hy is ideally placed to capture the scenes from the Director's box. All 10 outfield players had evolved through the youth ranks, so this was the triumphant culmination of many years of talent spotting and hard work.

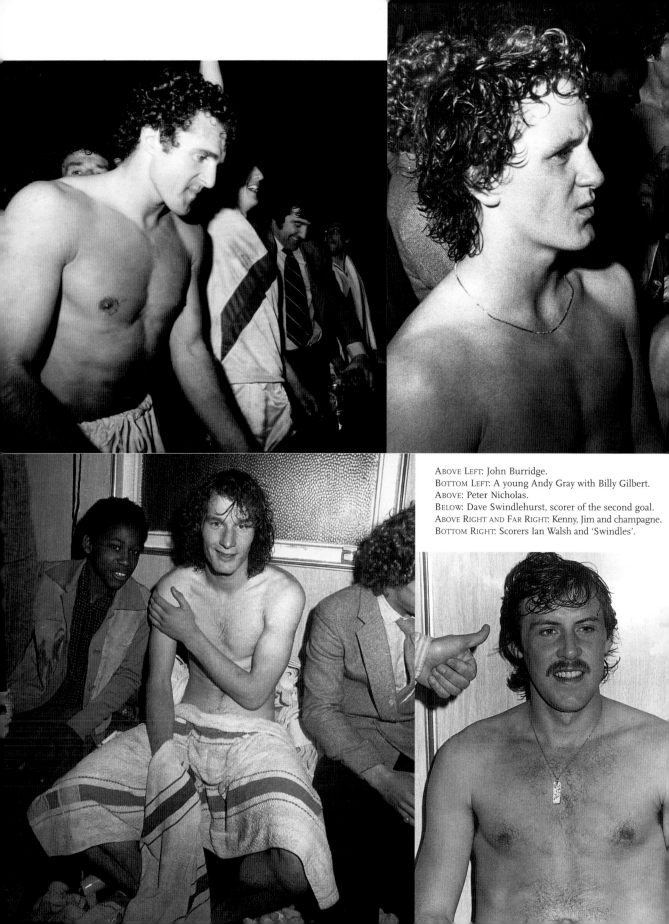

ABOVE LEFT: John Burridge.
BOTTOM LEFT: A young Andy Gray with Billy Gilbert.
ABOVE: Peter Nicholas.
BELOW: Dave Swindlehurst, scorer of the second goal.
ABOVE RIGHT AND FAR RIGHT: Kenny, Jim and champagne.
BOTTOM RIGHT: Scorers Ian Walsh and 'Swindles'.

LEFT: Hinshelwood and Walsh.
BOTTOM LEFT: Hy captures the back end of the celebrations.
ABOVE: Paul and Rita savour the moment in the Director's Box.

BELOW: Amongst others, Steve Lovell, Bob Horn, and David Fry celebrate.
RIGHT: Proud supporter Charlie Elsden, with Peter Nicholas.

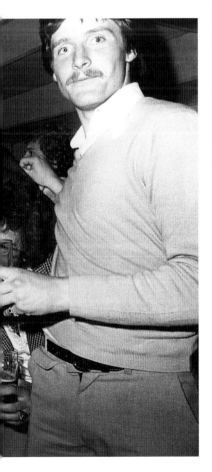

ABOVE AND MIDDLE LEFT: Burnley '83 and another Welsh Ian – this time Ian Edwards, brings another nail-biting season to a dramatic finale with an 83rd minute goal.
BOTTOM LEFT: Ron Noades checks the Timex. Above and Below: 4 years and 6 days on and

Burnley players leave the Selhurst pitch to another invasion.
TOP RIGHT: Relief.
RIGHT: Manager Mullery with scorer Edwards. Ian Edwards' fine Palace finale wrote him into the record books.

LEFT AND BELOW: An interesting comparison with the jubilant dressing-room scenes after the '79 game. Gary Locke, Jerry Murphy and Jim Cannon (below) experience a mixture of exhaustion and relief, and there's no champagne in sight this time.

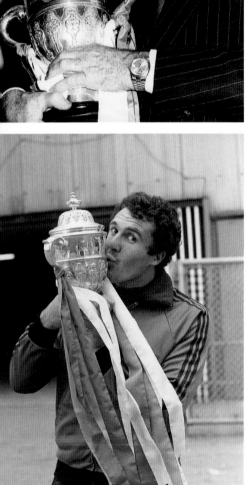

FAR LEFT: Ray Bloye (above) and John Burridge (below) pictured nursing the original 2nd Division Championship Trophy.

ABOVE LEFT: The inaugural 1st Division Championship Trophy with Manager Alan Smith and Ron Noades.

BOTTOM LEFT: John Burridge (and friends) in front of the Old Stand.

ABOVE: Tony Taylor, a mainstay of our first spell in the top flight, claims his just reward, The Glaziers Club Player of the Year Trophy.

ABOVE RIGHT: Gizza kiss then, son! Al 'n' Pete – born to compete.

RIGHT: Two fine gents... John Jackson presents Geoff Thomas with the Lifeline Player of the Year Trophy.

SPIT'N POLISH

ABOVE AND ABOVE RIGHT: JC (Jim Cannon, that is) blesses his 'holy cup'.

RIGHT: Mark Bright with the Lifeline Player of the Year award.

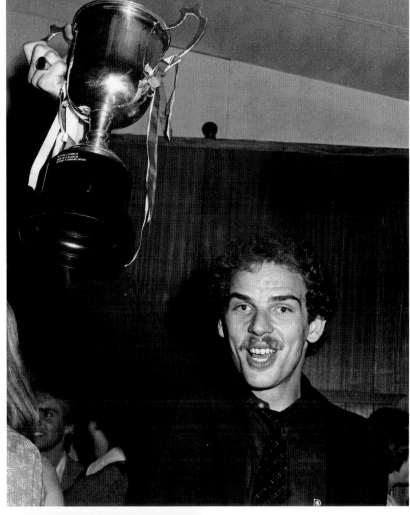

ABOVE AND BELOW LEFT: Paul Hinshelwood was Player of the Year in consecutive years in the top flight.

LEFT: Elaine Sansom caps a fine season for Kenny in '79.

ABOVE: The Bells Whisky Manager of the
Month award is usually cursed.
BELOW: Johnny 'Salad' Salako with the Young
Player of the Year award. A masterclass in
how to really show off a trophy.
BELOW RIGHT: The ever-effervescent Malcolm
Allison and Peter Taylor.

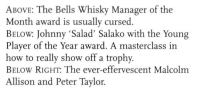

ABOVE AND ABOVE RIGHT: John Jackson & Roy Barry were both awarded the Away Travel Player of the Year Trophy.

RIGHT: Alan Mullery – possibly the biggest Cup he's ever won?

OPPOSITE: Geoff Thomas in a League fixture against Blackburn.
ABOVE: David Burke, a left back with a long throw.
LEFT: Wright-eous stuff against Huddersfield.
BELOW: Gavin Nebbeling slides in.

Above Left: Phil Barber in space.

Bottom Left: Eddie 'The Eagle' McGoldrick in full flight on the wing.

Left: Andy Thorn – "Is that you, Hy?"

Above: Neil Redfearn leaps with a Manchester City opponent.

BELOW: Mark Bright – poise and control against Manchester City. Ian Wright looks on.

ABOVE RIGHT: Tony Finnigan attempts The Mitsubishi Half-Time Challenge!

RIGHT: Two Johns – Salako and Humphrey.

OPPOSITE AND ABOVE: Alan Pardew scores 'a quickie' (see the clock) against Manchester City, one week before the F.A. Cup Final.

LEFT: Richard Shaw in a chase against Chelsea. Great scoreline.

BELOW: 'Brightie' up against Forest's Steve Chettle.

CLOCKWISE FROM LEFT: Big Mal; Billy Gilbert (with Ricky Rogers of Almo); Don Rogers; Vince Hilaire.

ABOVE AND FAR RIGHT: Kenny Sansom.

LEFT AND FAR RIGHT (ABOVE): Mel Blyth.

RIGHT, ABOVE AND BELOW: Jim Cannon,
joined (below) by Dave Swindlehurst.

DEDICATED FOLLOWERS OF...

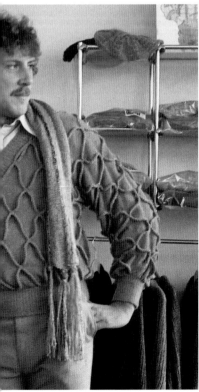

DEDICATED FOLLOWERS OF...

LEFT: Billy 'no socks' Gilbert with Steve Lovell.

BELOW: The 'Purley' King, Kenny Sansom.

RIGHT: Paul Hinshelwood's much deserved testimonial year. 'Are you sure those aren't forged, Sir!'

DEDICATED FOLLOWERS OF...

ABOVE: Big Mal plays a slide-rule pass.

RIGHT: Hy seems to prefer to focus on George Best than Mal. George is modelling Palace's 'Real Madrid' away kit.

BELOW: George's team line up at Selhurst. The super-skilled Frank Worthington is standing far right.

BELOW RIGHT: A Top Ten XI, featuring, among others, Micky Most, John Peel, Jess Conrad, David 'Diddy' Hamilton and Jim Davidson.

ABOVE: A part-reunion of the England World Cup winning team from '66. Back row, l-r: Ray Wilson, Bobby Charlton, Bobby Moore, Jack Charlton, Ron Springett, George Cohen, Gordon Banks, Martin Peters and (A.N.Other). Front row, l-r: Roger Hunt, Ian Callaghan, Jimmy Greaves and Geoff Hurst.

BELOW: Kevin 'The Godfather' O'Shea (front row, 2nd from right) was the driving force behind the Top Ten XI, who played to raise money for charities. Among others here are cricketer Geoff Arnold (3rd from left, back row) and the renowned Len Chatterton (front row, middle).

TESTIMONIALS & REUNIONS

FAR LEFT, TOP: George Graham takes the lads to the dogs. Frank McLintock (centre) is the interloper amongst the Palace stars.

FAR LEFT, BOTTOM: The annual Cardiac Arrest Challenge Cup between The Glaziers Club (in the sash) and the Vice President's (in the stripes) always produced outstandingly witty pen-pictures.

ABOVE LEFT: Back together again for 'Jimbo' Cannon's 2nd testimonial are Ian Evans, John Burridge, Jim himself and Dave Swindlehurst.

MARTIN HINSHELWOOD'S TESTIMONIAL.

ABOVE: Son Danny meets Nookie Bear.

BELOW LEFT: After this, his final game at Selhurst, Martin leaves the field for a future in management.

BELOW: Martin with Diana Dors.

ABOVE AND LEFT: Jim Cannon's first testimonial game brought together the cream of black British football talent. 'Captain' Vince Hilaire's XI helped produce a memorably entertaining goal-fest.

RIGHT: Hy organised this 'Football-Aid' friendly which pre-dated Live Aid, with Linda Lusardi adding the glamour. Any familiar faces amongst 'The Westminster Wobblers'? Well, there's a diminutive John Prescott (back row).

FAR RIGHT: Also on the left wing, but likewise often drifting toward the centre, Neil Kinnock sits in the dugout after being deselected during the game.

ITY FOOTBALL MATCH

Sunday May 12th 1985
in aid of Ethiopian Famine Relief

THE      A
AMENTARY XI v. CELEBRITY XI
(Westminster Wobblers)

Palace F.C., Selhurst Park    K.O. 3.00pm

ADMISSION 50p

Linda Lusardi pictured at the House of Commons

REUNION. INDIVIDUAL PORTRAITS, ANTI-CLOCKWISE FROM TOP LEFT:
Geoff Truett 57-62; Terry Long 55-73; Tony Collins 57-59; Eddie Werge 61-
66; Alan Stephenson 62-68; Peter Burridge 62-65;Bobby Kellard 63-65 &
71-72; Jim Cannon 70-88; Alan Pinkney 69-74; Phil Hoadley 69-71;
Bobby Woodruff 66-69.

GROUP PORTRAIT, ABOVE: Kneeling in Foreground (l-r): Dave Madden, Jim Cannon, Gavin Nebbeling and Nicky Chatterton. Standing (l-r): David Payne, Eddie Werge, Mark Lazarus, Brian Wood, Alan Pinkney (back), Bobby Kellard (front), Keith Smith, Dennis Uphill, Tony Collins, Geoff Truett, Terry Long, Brian Whitehouse, Peter Berry, Vic Rouse, Bobby Woodruff, Danny Light, Alan Stephenson and Phil Hoadley.

| | |
|---|---|
| **PRESENTATION COPIES TO:** | |

PRESENTATION COPIES TO:
Crystal Palace Football Club
The Football Association
The Football League
The National Football Museum

Hy and CPfCP wish to thank the following

# SUBSCRIBERS

*(Note: date represents year of first game attended)*

| | |
|---|---|
| David Payne | 55 |
| Tony Taylor | 68 |
| Jack Edwards | 49 |
| Paul Hinshelwood | 71 |
| Albert Zealey 1904-92 | 14 |
| The Noades Family | 81 |
| Rez Halil | 84 |
| Ian King | 66 |
| Alexander Booth | 67 |
| Mark Booth | 71 |
| Lee Dawkins | 70 |
| Ron R. Daughtry | 68 |
| Steve Carlton | 60 |
| Ron Gadd | 68 |
| Bill Lazard B.A. N.D.D. | 50 |
| Chris Winter | 68 |
| In memory – Lenny Hill | 68 |
| Jim Ryan | 64 |
| Peter Watts | 53 |
| Nick Wilkins | 58 |
| Ian Paul Eldridge | 73 |
| Andy Clark | 67 |
| Max Grosse | 63 |
| Pat & Richard Fencott | 54 |
| Michael J. Dubus | 46 |
| Victor Hillary | 74 |
| Ian Jeive | 69 |
| John Thompson | 64 |
| Barry Stevens | 57 |
| Ralph Smith | 59 |
| Darrell S.M. Bourne | 60 |
| Gerry Coll | 71 |
| Ian Chatters | 73 |
| Jordan Paul Iles | 98 |

**LEFT:** How could this book end with anything else but... High Money.

| | |
|---|---|
| Steve Purcell | 68 |
| Paul Lahert | 71 |
| David Lahert | 71 |
| Matthew Davis | 78 |
| Steve Adamson | 69 |
| Jim Buttress | 54 |
| Tony Tookey | 68 |
| Jim Davis & Family | 68 |
| Pete & Chris Gee | 69 |
| Andrew Fishleigh | 61 |
| Andy Tipping | 71 |
| Susan Edwards | 68 |
| The Broadway Boys | 68 |
| Barry Graney | 72 |
| Terry O'Neil | 42 |
| Graeme Stobart | 72 |
| Neil Eldridge | 65 |
| Neil Simpson | 60 |
| David J. Robinson | 55 |
| John Stanford | 70 |
| Kevin Day | 68 |
| Andrew Richard Smith | 86 |
| Michael Tompsett | 49 |
| Benjamin Tilly | 78 |
| Dominic Burrell | 69 |
| Bob Hall | 63 |
| Peter & Janet Lane | 47 |
| John & Steven Lane | 47 |
| Mark Gordon Skeens | 92 |
| Greg Roffey | 71 |
| Angela Vince | 65 |
| John Vince | 68 |
| Chris Conquest | 80 |
| Peter Conquest | 53 |
| Richard Furphy | 73 |
| John Clark | 61 |
| Mick Murphy | 58 |
| Jack Taylor | 94 |
| Nicholas & Jonathon Mole | 57 |
| Toni Skeet | 68 |
| Tony Tyrrell | 56 |
| Mark Tyrrell | 84 |
| Paul Newman | 59 |
| Colin Ferguson Duncan | 46 |
| Ivor Duncan | 75 |
| Phil Sutton-Jones | 63 |
| Darren Morgan | 80 |
| John A. Carter | 47 |
| Ian E. Baker | 67 |
| Matthew Skeats | 83 |
| Sam Musgrove | 47 |
| Simon McHardy | 91 |
| West Family, Basingstoke | 45 |
| Andrew Collins | 76 |
| Michael Hersey | 77 |

| | |
|---|---|
| David London | 87 |
| Johann Williams | 74 |
| Paul Fleury | 69 |
| Ben Fleury | 00 |
| Diana Cowell | 65 |
| Sue Duke | 89 |
| Ian & Viv McRae | 66 |
| Chris Richards | 60 |
| John Hall | 48 |
| Chris Hall | 85 |
| Kevin Kilbey | 67 |
| Dave Matthews | 60 |
| Roy Brideswell | 70 |
| Vince & Elliott Sexton | 72 |
| Sarah Coleman | 70 |
| Don Pettingale | 60 |
| B. V. Beswick | 45 |
| Alan Golding | 65 |
| Peter Johnson Moverman | 68 |
| Steve Way | 69 |
| Claire Cook | 97 |
| Luke & Ben Price | 69 |
| Peter Lewis Robinson | 80 |
| John Williams | 50 |
| Ron Westbrook | 61 |
| Mat Beecham | 80 |
| Denne Beecham | 48 |
| Ian Wilkinson & Family | 67 |
| Andy Carey | 77 |
| Denis Bylett | 54 |
| Paul & John Brieeon | 68 |
| Colin Belcher | 69 |
| Andrew Belcher | 73 |
| Phil Huffer | 75 |
| Michael Van-Boolen | 67 |
| Dermot Hennessy | 65 |
| John-Paul Theobald | 75 |
| Caroline Childs | 90 |
| Ian Lander | 69 |
| Rick Ballantine | 72 |
| Mike O'Neill | 90 |
| Mark Page | 88 |
| Les White | 56 |
| Robin Phipps | 56 |
| Kevin T. Connery | 79 |
| John Fahey | 73 |
| Sophia Price-Ross | 89 |
| G. Haywood | 68 |
| Graham Bell | 73 |
| Jeff Lewis | 75 |
| Mark Baker | 71 |
| Gary & Tracey Wallis | 75 |
| Keith & Tom Blackwell | 56 |
| Colin Howlett | 70 |
| Mike Tebbutt | 78 |

| | |
|---|---|
| Graham Axtell | 71 |
| Angus Gartshore | 99 |
| Richard Haynes | 78 |
| John Richardson | 69 |
| David Clark | 57 |
| Paul Clark | 77 |
| Mark Kelly | 68 |
| Paul Andrew Younger | 69 |
| Ben Oliver Younger | 00 |
| Robert Stephen Younger | 69 |
| Steve Brett | 58 |
| David Bonser | 69 |
| Michael Gylanders | 53 |
| Martin Cole | 68 |
| Eric Pudney | 35 |
| Grant Kelly | 66 |
| Roger Checkley | 58 |
| Paul O'Gorman | 65 |
| George Zeleny | 69 |
| Neil Duncanson | 69 |
| Mark Evetts | 71 |
| Martin John Smith | 78 |
| Peter Bright | 63 |
| Dave & Jan Simpson | 60 |
| Chris Wait | 65 |
| Brian Wait | 55 |
| Michael Tucker | 86 |
| William H.H. Davis | 66 |
| Leo McCann | 86 |
| Gavin Grossmith | 69 |
| Vincent & Gavin Griffiths | 72 |
| Daren Edwards | 78 |
| Phillip Mott | 66 |
| Paul Collins | 66 |
| John Roberts | 69 |
| Steve Parker | 67 |
| Nigel Povah | 68 |
| Jon Winbow | 80 |
| Rob Gordon | 63 |
| Richard Wilkes | 65 |
| Steve Francis | 69 |
| Paul Kelsey | 59 |
| Ronnie Puttock | 56 |
| Chris, James & Al Connor | 70 |
| Peter Eyers | 69 |
| Jim Barnes | 60 |
| Alan Gordon | 77 |
| John Gilmour | 74 |
| Neil Munro | 69 |
| Barry Llewellyn | 73 |
| Charles Bake | 69 |
| Phelim Slevin | 66 |
| Andrew Ward | 77 |
| Ashley Sayed | – |
| Graham White | 52 |

| Name | No. | Name | No. | Name | No. | Name | No. |
|---|---|---|---|---|---|---|---|
| David Shaw | 68 | James Patrick Durkin | 60 | Karen Muir | 65 | Alan Sach | 68 |
| John Addley | 72 | John & Sylvia Henty | 47 | Michael Moore | 58 | Mervyn F. D'Cruz | 68 |
| Sean Addley | 95 | Andrew & Marysia Henty | 71 | Jane Vigus | 66 | Paul Hilton | 90 |
| Jamie & Emma Seekings | 91 | John G. Axtell | 55 | Richard Goodman | 84 | Ros Poulson | 76 |
| Colin Vogt | 71 | Alan Lucking | 60 | Sarah Cushing | 96 | Neil Witherow | 70 |
| Steve Blakesley | 69 | MacDonald's-Shortlands | 84 | Paul Jeanes | 71 | Tristan Hawkins | 83 |
| Steve Crisp | 71 | Steve McAllister | 66 | Dan 'Magoo' Barlow | 78 | Jonathon Smith | 63 |
| Mrs Beryl Smith | 49 | Graham & Daniel May | 69 | Emma Dodd | 90 | James Fisher | 63 |
| Mark Holder | 43 | John Coventon | 63 | Ian Brazil | 72 | Dave & Vanessa Wheeler | 71 |
| Phillip Holder | 76 | David Coventon | 71 | Yoshi Uchida | 79 | Daniel Gordon | 75 |
| Derrick Emmett | 71 | Jude & Sarah Coventon | 88 | Justin Cairns | 80 | Carl Davis | 75 |
| Arthur John Green | 47 | The Marks'– Burgess Hill | 76 | Diane Horan | 91 | John Davis | 73 |
| Clive Smith | 68 | Darren De Souza | 84 | Matthew Dodds | 78 | Richard Kenyon | 78 |
| John R. Ramage | 87 | Ian Rubie | 67 | Richard Learner | 68 | Patrick Kenyon | 78 |
| Brian Rayner | 72 | Peter Sutton | 59 | Oliver James Shaw | 65 | Nick Kenyon | 85 |
| Janet Claire Gates | 76 | Trevor Prockter | 65 | Peter Campbell | 01 | Nick Smith | 85 |
| Ted Gates | 48 | Peter Dodge | 71 | Roger Wiggs | 75 | Chris Wright | 79 |
| Graham Saunders | 63 | Brian Simpson | 49 | Martyn Browne | 83 | Alan Wright | 57 |
| Paul Christopher Mosely | 88 | Dave Pamphilon | 70 | Robert Riviere | 72 | Christopher Hood | 76 |
| Chris Bonser | 66 | Derek Cooper | 69 | Derek Driver | 39 | Malcolm Ashman | 87 |
| Mark Sherin | 78 | Dave Lewis | 79 | Reub Warren | 69 | Jason Flynn | 86 |
| Tom Maslona | 81 | John Styles | 59 | Clive Austin | 69 | Joe Grech | 70 |
| Dave Burchell | 63 | Paul Styles | 78 | David Weller | 77 | John Horlock | 53 |
| Stewart Baldwin | 86 | Peter Waller | 59 | Robert Tolfrey | 64 | Paul Lipton Rose | 65 |
| Tony Lahert | 88 | John Collard | 48 | Peter Hurn | 62 | Martyn | 69 |
| Ian Weller | 56 | Hazel Young | 69 | Alan Lee | 57 | Bob Matthews | 66 |
| Ken Priestley | 54 | Clifford Joseph Lambdon | 59 | Peter Hayes | 57 | Morgan Michie | 70 |
| Matthew Barker | 87 | Graham Johnson | 68 | Steve Scanlon | 68 | Michael O'Keefe | 70 |
| Iain Barker | 58 | Julia Todd | 67 | Tony Brown | 59 | Rob Pearce | 88 |
| Denys Barker | 35 | Stephen Hubble | 74 | Nick Redman | 86 | Helen Myska | 92 |
| Jeff & Lewis Woodard | 73 | Roger Starbuck & Family | 56 | Steve Everest | 61 | Dr Danny White | 70 |
| Paul Moren | 74 | Terry Morley | 61 | Peter Redman | 86 | Pete Wylie | 80 |
| Ian Spires – | – | Chetan Mistry | 91 | John 'Statto' McBride | 42 | Paul Stevens | 59 |
| Oliver Frankham | 79 | Carl Skinner | 88 | Pete & Alice – The Eagles | 88 | Mike Welchman | 50 |
| Bert Peploe | 38 | Mick Skinner | 70 | Graeme Ley | 67 | Sue Maisey | 90 |
| Edward Rice | 71 | Edward Quelch | 52 | Dean Smythe | 69 | Roger West | 61 |
| Stephen Barry Glazer | 54 | John Cartland | 48 | David Brian Sparrow | 46 | Daniel Simmons | 79 |
| Martin and Rachel Glassborow | 59 | The Ricketts Family | 48 | Brian John Sparrow | 76 | Jonathon Selwyn | 72 |
| Laura Glassborow | 95 | Steven Pilbro | 57 | Stephen Sherriff | 66 | Alan Selwyn | 70 |
| Sarah Kingsbury | 93 | Trevor Baker | 69 | Paul Firmage | 63 | Tim Grewal | 80 |
| Alan Lee | 63 | Jill Clarke | 69 | Len Cheesman | 51 | John & James Daniel Gunn | 76 |
| Trevor & Kathy Clark | 58 | Ian T. Richardson | 63 | Frank Cates | 48 | James Taylor-Nye | 80 |
| Julia Duplock | 69 | John Bailey | 55 | James & Stephen Grice | 70 | Richard Fernandez | 89 |
| Andy, Jen, Ian & Jo Parry | 58 | Bill Boakes | 44 | Danny Foley | 66 | Nigel Moran | 77 |
| Ian Dawes | 73 | Sean Walton-Carroll | 73 | Kevin Spooner | 79 | Jim Moran | 73 |
| Peter Dawes | 73 | Claire Walton-Carroll | 85 | Peter 'Rocky' Evans | 76 | Phil, Aisling, Ronan Smith | 72 |
| Stephen Marshe Ball | 58 | Steve Read | 77 | Steve Marsh | 71 | Karl Frearson | 58 |
| Maurice Soden | 65 | The Dockery Family | 71 | Mrs Samantha Smith | 83 | Trevor Harrod | 58 |
| Gary Yandle | 76 | Martin L. Walshe | 74 | Dominic Fifield | 85 | Nigel Wearing | 77 |
| Lunn & Melody's (IRE) | 50 | Simon & Helen Bond | 82 | Gary&Jack Rendell | 70 | Caroline McGovern | 71 |
| Jonny Edser | 89 | Clare Howard | 80 | Jeffrey Carter | 56 | Peter Johnson | 72 |
| Roger Gagen | 56 | Matthew & Eliza Bond | 99 | Ron & Bob Reeves | 61 | Geoff & Dan Skipsey | 93 |
| Graham Steers | 58 | Peter Carpenter | 71 | Martin Lockton | 53 | Clyde Dempster | 70 |
| Chris Hyland | 68 | John, Luke, Lucy Roberts | 79 | Luke Hooper | 94 | David Joyce | 86 |
| Ian Brockman | 76 | Bill Philpott | 52 | Mark Stewart | 76 | David Bennett | 73 |

| Name | | Name | | Name | | Name | |
|---|---|---|---|---|---|---|---|
| Pam & Lynne Kyle | 68 | Adam Edgar | 88 | Graham Bell | 70 | Kevin Newman | 87 |
| Richard Johns | 46 | Richard Coombs | 73 | Ian Warrilow | 70 | Aidan Devaney | 73 |
| Julie, Dan, Beaky, Barnett | 70 | Laurence Sullivan | 70 | Kim Manson | 70 | Barry Couldrick | 68 |
| Lynda Stevens | 69 | George & Roger Arnold | 78 | Tony & Sylvia Warrilow | 70 | Graham Maskell | 64 |
| Norman Barnett | 25 | Stephen Arnold | 78 | Jimmy Speed | 71 | Dean Hollingsworth | 79 |
| The Morris Family | 65 | Roger Dickson | 57 | Michael Sell | 72 | Roberto Blenman | 68 |
| Graham Wilson | 56 | Richard Gribble | 59 | Mark English (Belgium) | 73 | Dave King | 79 |
| Tim Marshall | 70 | Eddie & Lisa Chaplin | 71 | Chris M. Barnes | 71 | Malcolm Harmes | 99 |
| Dean O'Hara | 75 | Derek Collison | 72 | Michael Evans | 70 | Hayden Gregory | 96 |
| Dave Grant | 75 | Adam Bentley | 79 | George W. Elliott | 72 | Julian Radcliffe | 83 |
| Matthew Morgan | 87 | Colin & Sue Darnell | 52 | Andy Webb | 76 | Karl Cressey | 99 |
| Lee McCann | 89 | John & Simon Higgins | 72 | Amanda & Robbie Breach | 68 | Ian Cressey | 59 |
| Ross McCann | 89 | Tony Gee, Anthony Crook | 91 | Graham Carter | 80 | Alan White | 64 |
| Simon Woods | 86 | Joe Burek | 69 | John Carter | 49 | Louise Court | 68 |
| Phil Colvin | 77 | Brian Stotten | 60 | Raymond Carter | 24 | Laurie Dahl | 79 |
| Gareth Limpenny | 76 | Ramzi Musallam | 72 | Pauline & Peter Hare | 68 | Mark & Justin Champagne | 81 |
| Neil Black | 76 | John McGovern | 63 | Nathan Rose | 85 | Matthew Austin | 72 |
| Andy Southern | 63 | Peter M. Millen | 58 | Eric Moore | 65 | Raymond Austin | 41 |
| Stuart Dunbar | 70 | John F. Holroyd | 54 | Douglas Andrew Symon | 93 | Bill Nighy | 49 |
| Graham Perrin | 80 | Peter Walker | 45 | Graham M. Cross | 54 | Joshua Nighy | 02 |
| Martin Pelosi | 80 | Rowenna Walker | 78 | Martin Thomas | 64 | Martin Nighy | 72 |
| Paul Gear | 80 | James Walker | 37 | Peter Thomas | 46 | Martin Joseph Nighy | 79 |
| Richard Barnes | 69 | Barrie Dunning | 65 | Nigel King | 70 | Andrew Maybin | 87 |
| Andy Kieselack | 68 | Dave Morgan | 63 | Anthony King | 83 | Robert Maybin | 89 |
| William Block | 81 | Cathy Churchman | 86 | David King | 87 | Colin Vidler | 54 |
| J.T. Sutch | 04 | Jane Filler | 89 | Cliff Arch | 69 | Mike Clemens | 57 |
| David Kemp | 68 | James White | 97 | Gwen Lamb | 54 | Roger Mitchell | 60 |
| Martin Filer | 84 | Michael Knoth | 72 | Stephen Lamb | 76 | Del Grant | 71 |
| Bob Lock | 72 | Jeff Butler | 69 | Brian Ian Gary John Davis | 86 | Ferdie Gould | 04 |
| Jonathon Lock | 02 | Rob Butler | 71 | Mark John Smith | 74 | Graham Ardley | 63 |
| David Brown | 72 | Terry Parratt | 70 | Neil Spires | 77 | David Watts | 55 |
| Ted Grant | 36 | Stephen Saunders | 69 | Jim Porter | 60 | David Green | 59 |
| Paul Grant | 65 | Paul Wilson | 86 | Simon Hepher | 73 | David Williams | 68 |
| Tim McDonogh | 74 | Peter Birch | 60 | Adrian Black | 68 | John Williams | 63 |
| Alex Chrysostomou | 81 | Peter Appleton | 69 | Mike Kimberley | 68 | Chris Banner | 65 |
| D.J. Erny | 57 | Craig Parker | 88 | Olly Olatunji | 75 | Andy Middleton | 65 |
| Paul Oliver | 68 | Beth & Chris Hughes | 85 | Scott Joseph Walker | 72 | Keith Bezodis | 59 |
| Mary Meehan | 67 | Alan Mills | 64 | Christopher Mead | 86 | Martin Knight | 68 |
| Timothy Mears | 68 | Terry Turner | 77 | Jack Holloway | 73 | Martin Money | 71 |
| Stanley Churchmann | 65 | Gary Lines | 85 | Grant Keir | 69 | Ellie & Harrison Money | 00 |
| Kenneth Quinn | 41 | Graham Attaway | 69 | Terence Joseph Perrin | 76 | Lisa Smith (Money) | 76 |
| Jeremy Walker | 71 | Alex Kerr | – | Ian Howe | 69 | Alex & Jack Smith | 05 |
| Robert Hinson | 77 | Scott Kerr | – | Jack Ford | 88 | Anthony Money | 71 |
| Simon Moll | 72 | Robert Gale | 78 | Richard Ogilvie-Taylor | 96 | Tyler & Chandler Money | 00 |
| James Charlton | 75 | Peter Lane | 79 | Stuart Norris | 63 | Stuart Money | 71 |
| Mark Charlton | 79 | Derek Prescott | 51 | David Norris | 89 | Isobel & Millie Money | 05 |
| Anthony Charlton | 51 | Chris Harris | 64 | Brian Halfacre | 58 | Lissi Harling | – |
| David Charlton | 86 | David Dudding | 78 | Clive Vurnum | 48 | Colleen Murphy(Money)USA | – |
| Liz Grimsey | 59 | The Davis Gang | 71 | Nicholas Harling | 60 | Robert McEachern USA | – |
| The Slater's | 72 | Peter Manning | 59 | Steve John Sewell | 69 | Ben Hardisty | 72 |
| Dave Sue Jack Matt Ryan | 76 | Gordon Brunton | 61 | James Simmonds | 77 | Terje Riis | 76 |
| Tony, Joe & Mason West | 74 | David Higgins | 71 | Adrian Glendinning | 72 | Bjarne Servold | 81 |
| Steve Smith | 62 | Daniel Frewing | 81 | Paul Smith | 75 | Norman Turpin | 61 |
| Steve & Oliver Bostwick | 58 | Brian King | 49 | James Naylor | 75 | Don Madgwick | 76 |
| Rick Bates | 83 | Leslie L. Dye | 53 | Mike Thorn | 69 | Hy Money | 71 |

SO GLAD YOU'RE MINE 11-5-79